MYTHS *of the*
NORTH
AMERICAN
INDIANS

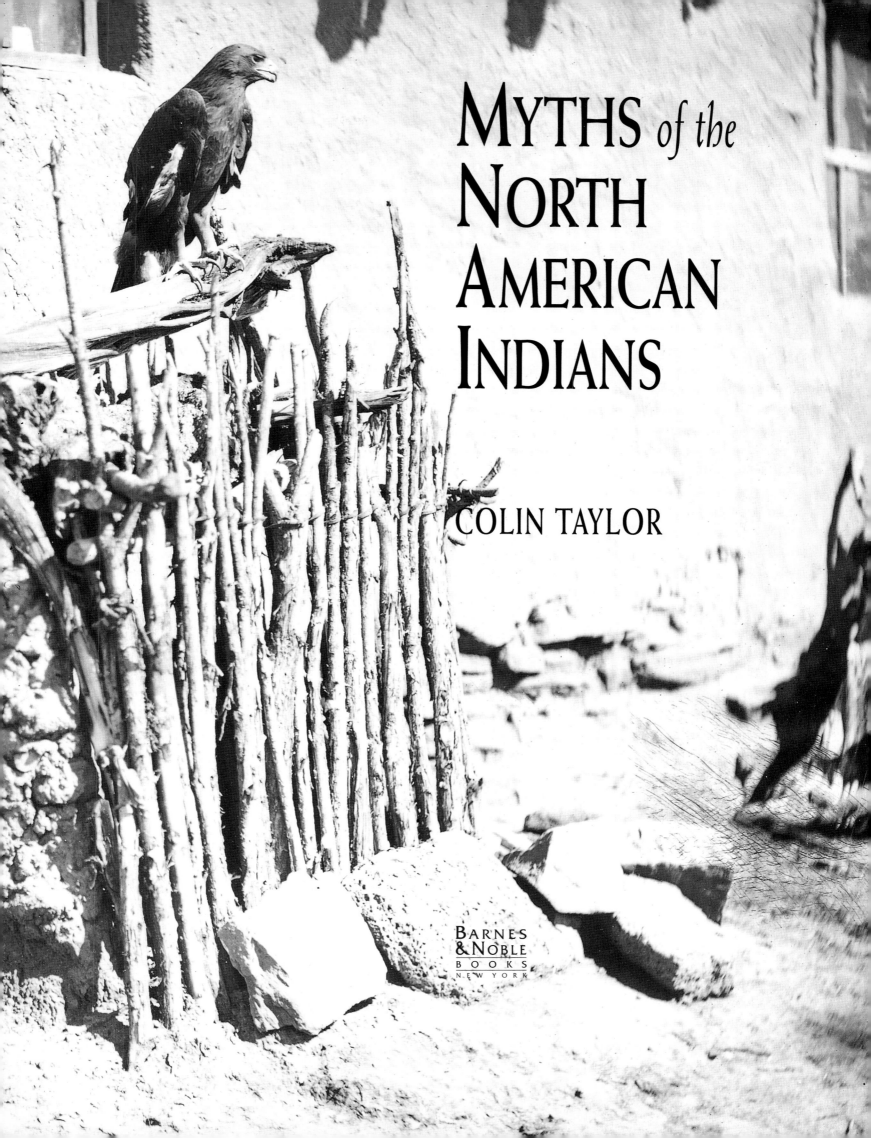

MYTHS *of the* NORTH AMERICAN INDIANS

COLIN TAYLOR

BARNES & NOBLE BOOKS
NEW YORK

ACKNOWLEDGEMENTS

Colin Taylor would like to thank Paula Fleming for all her work and also Karen Stafford and the staff of Calmann and King for their courtesy and support during the production of this volume.

FRONTISPIECE *A Zuni man leans against an eagle cage made of adobe and wooden stakes.*
The young eagles were captured from their nests and kept in cages such as this.
The plumage – particularly the tail and feathers – were highly prized for use in ceremonies as the eagle
was considered a highly sacred bird in most Native American cultural areas, figuring prominently in their
rituals and symbolism. Both shed and plucked feathers were used – the bird was not generally killed.
Photograph by J. K. Hillers, Zuni Pueblo, New Mexico, 1879.

This edition published by Barnes & Noble Inc.,
by arrangement with Laurence King Publishing.
1995 Barnes & Noble Books

Introduction and chapter introductions copyright
© 1995 Calmann and King Ltd

ISBN 1-56619-838-0

Designed and typeset by Karen Stafford, DQP, London
Photo research by Paula Fleming
Printed in Italy

Contents

Introduction

A GREAT DEAL OF NORTH AMERICAN INDIAN MYTHOLOGY centered around myths of creation, hunting, farming, the powers of the cosmic forces that created the universe, and the great terrestrial forces of fire, thunder, lightning, hail and storm. In addition, many myths and legends derived from a perceived rapport with animals, which might become an individual's guide and protector. There was also a recognition that certain plants were valuable for medicinal purposes and these too were given a place in mythological lore.

There is little doubt that the mythology of the North American Indians was strongly intertwined with their religion and that it can be broadly separated into two groups: that which concerned the tribe as a whole and that which related to the individual. There was a great emphasis on the existence of an overwhelming and mysterious higher power – such as Wakanda, Manitou and Orenda of the Siouan, Algonquian and Iroquoian linguistic groups. In many ceremonies and myths, recognition was given to such powers – often at the expense of great physical and mental effort – in the hope that they could be harnessed for the good of the tribe or individual.

Most of the myths in this volume derive from the *Legends and Lore of the American Indians* (New York, 1993), edited by Terri Hardin, who brought together some three hundred myths and legends of the North American Indian. A few additional myths have been included to give balance and to illustrate the flavor or origins of some important ceremonies, such as the Lakota Sun Dance and O-kee-pa ceremony of the Mandan (Chapter 6) or to give further insights into the creation myths and the tribal legends (Chapters 1, 2, and 5): sources for these are identified in the relevant chapters.

The myths fall into six thematic categories, ranging from those relating to creation and origins to the mythology and lore that was often used to describe the development of tribal ceremonies and customs. It should be appreciated that the full meaning of a myth may be obscured in the process of translation or by our lack of knowledge of the culture of the tribe who related it, since many date from at least the nineteenth century – some much earlier. Thus, as one recent field-worker observed when researching among the indigenous people of the Northwest Territories (Northern Canada): 'We became aware of a number of barriers. The foremost being that of language. While conversing in English with the most articulate people, or speaking through a translator, a certain sense developed – an almost sad longing – that the English language is not equipped to communicate the concepts and nuances of another world view' (Irving and Harper, p. 39). Such difficulties need to be kept in mind when reading the myths that follow.

The selection has been such that all the nine cultural areas of North America are represented. These areas are a useful way of classifying the lifestyles of the people who lived in the various regions and are shown on the map (pp. 170-71). The cultures were very strongly influenced by environment, although distinctions gradually merged at the boundaries: thus, for example the Prairie tribes of the Eastern Plains exhibited both Woodland and Plains cultural traits.

THE SOUTHWEST

A region of arid deserts, green river valleys, and high stark snow-topped mountains. It is largely defined by the present-day states of New Mexico and Arizona together with the northern regions of Mexico with slight extensions into Texas, Utah and Colorado. While there is strong evidence of human habitation at least 12,000 years ago, the cultures of the peoples known to the first Europeans – the Spaniards arrived in the middle of the sixteenth century – fully flowered around 900 AD. By this latter date these so-called Puebloan and Piman tribes – descendants of the ancient Anasazi (a Navajo name meaning 'Old Peoples'), Hohokam and Mogollon cultures – shared the same culture in varying degrees. For example, they grew beans, squash, varicolored corn, cotton, and tobacco and produced handsome coiled, polished and painted pottery, while their clothing consisted of blankets and other garments that were woven on tall, upright looms. They also abandoned the early styles of cliff dwellings and pit houses, the Puebloans living in large communal habitations made of stones plastered with adobe, and the Pimans in dome-shaped, thatched structured of poles, brush and earth, the door of which always faced east.

About 1400, other groups arrived from the north; these were Athapaskan-speaking peoples, now known as the Navajo and Apaches. A whole string of pueblos along the Rio Grande valley was abandoned for fear of them, and the Navajo and Apaches gradually filtered into the Southwest, where they became semi-nomads. The Navajo mainly lived in earth-covered hogans, the Apaches in *wickiups*, a type of brush arbor often thatched with bear grass. These late arrivals adopted much of the culture of the Southwest but, with the acquisition of sheep from the Spaniards, the Navajo replaced cotton with wool. They became skilled weavers of blankets and, later, in the 1850s, they learned from the Mexicans how to work silver, combining it with the turquoise of the region to produce elaborate and much coveted jewelry.

Thus, the mythology of the tribes in this region is a mixture of tales: some are flavored by those of the ancient indigenous people, on to which have been superimposed those of the newly emerged Puebloan and Piman cultures, together with those of the late arrivals, Athapaskan, Navajo and Apache. The selection reflects this difference, for example, the narrative of the Zuni Sky God contrasts markedly with that of the Navajo's Black God (Chapter 4).

THE SOUTHEAST

The majority of this region falls within the broad coastal plains that border the Atlantic at the east and the Gulf of Mexico to the west, and the area encompasses most of present-day Alabama, Georgia, Caroline, Tennessee, and Florida. The tribes occupying it in the

PREVIOUS PAGE *Woman and young girl wearing dress and costume. Flathead Indian Reservation, western Montana, probably photographed by Major Lee Moorhouse about 1900. The Mission Mountains can just be seen in the background. The costume worn by the woman and the horse regalia are typical of this tribe for the period. Note particularly the high pommel and cantle saddles, the horse chest ornament, and the beaded cradle carried by the horse on the left.*

The Apache, Buck Kehlh, photographed by Edward S. Curtis about 1906. The Apache were of an Athapaskan linguistic stock, who called themselves Dine 'people' – an ancient Subarctic term. They were divided into a number of tribal groups, the best known of which were the Mescaleros, Jicarillas, White Mountain, and Mimbres. This man wears a typical Apache war cap of buckskin, embellished with cut feathers

nineteenth century were the product of a long period of change after the first contacts with Europeans, which occurred as early as 1513 when the Spanish explorer, Ponce de Leon, landed in Florida. By about 1700, the region was inhabited mainly by Muskogean-speaking peoples, such as the Creek, Seminole (an offshoot of the Creek), Chickasaw, Choctaw, and Natchez. However, to the north lived the Cherokee who spoke a language related to the Iroquois. (The Creek, Chickasaw, Choctaw, Cherokee, and Seminole were classified in government records during the nineteenth century as the 'Five Civilized Tribes'). The land occupied by these various tribes was threaded with rivers and streams and provided a bountiful food supply.

In common with most hunting tribes, the Southeastern Indians believed in many animal and plant spirits, which were thought to embody a mysterious force that pervaded all of nature. Above them were the spirits of the air and earth and superior to them all was the so-called Master of Breath. As is related in the Muskogean Creation story (Chapter 1) the latter was credited with the creation of man from the clay that surrounded His abode.

The Choctaw myth relating to the Deluge (Chapter 1) underlines the Southeastern belief that it behoves man to respect all these spirits and indicates the consequences if this is ignored. A message that runs through this style of myth is one of renewal, as is reflected in the solemn cleansing ceremonies of these tribes, where individuals were scratched to draw blood and then purified themselves with an emetic – often referred to as the 'Black Drink'.

PLATEAU AND BASIN

In the nineteenth century this cultural area comprised the region from central British Columbia, south to Nevada and Utah; towards the north it crossed the Continental Divide into northwestern Montana and in the south, the Rocky Mountains to the east and the Sierra Nevada to the west. Much of the Plateau culture depended on the two great rivers, the Columbia and the Fraser, salmon and other fish being a vital food for many of the tribes who lived there. In addition, the lush valleys provided ample forage for the numerous game. However, as one moves south, the magnitude and importance of these rivers progressively declines and in the regions now called Nevada and Utah, sagebrush and saltbrush deserts dominate. Here, in the Great Basin – so-called because no rivers drained from it to the sea – lived the Digger Indians, a resourceful people, so named because of their great dependence on wild vegetables and roots, which they prised out of the ground with sharp pointed sticks. The mythology of these people reflects their relative poverty and lacks the richness of imagination found in most other cultural areas. Thus, the Basin tribes had prosaic animal tales, which were often obscene, while myths relating to their origins, go no further than to say that the world was put in good order by Coyote and Wolf.

All the Indians in this region were semi-nomadic and in the early nineteenth century contained some twenty-five tribes belonging to at least two main language stocks – Salishan and Sahaptin. Here lived the Nez Perce, Walla Walla, Cayuse, Umatilla, Flathead, and Kutenai, horse-rich tribes who traded animals far and wide. Many lived in communal dwellings, compartmentalized to accommodate individual families. Several, such as the Nez Perce, Kutenai, and Flathead, frequently used the tipi, particularly on their expeditions to the Plains.

In this predominantly non-agricultural region, there are few references to the womb of the earth; instead, there is an abundance of myths relating to animals, particularly Coyote who, in the form of Trickster, is often described as being selfish, greedy, and clever,

Zuni Raindance photographed by Vroman at the Pueblo in New Mexico in 1899. Performed by the Kokkoksi or 'Good Kachinas', they are shown here probably on their way to the plaza after a pilgrimage to the Sacred Lake. Raindances were performed throughout the summer months at Zuni: the costume – of which the long hair was particularly distinctive – was probably copied by the Hopi for their Angakchina or 'Long–haired Kachinas'.

demonstrating to mankind – by his blunders and outlandish escapades – how *not* to live. Coyote was also a creator, and elements of this are touched on in the Flathead myth, where Coyote kills a giant by cutting up its heart (Chapter 5), while the benefits of pleasing the animal spirits are suggested by the Nez Perce myth relating to the Beaver's role in bringing fire to the tribe (Chapter 2).

THE PLAINS

This great flat region stretches from the base of the Rocky Mountains to the Mississippi and north from the North Saskatchewan River in present-day Alberta almost to the Gulf of Mexico. It can be divided into three main parts. In the west are the foothills of the Rockies, somewhat barren and rugged; in the east are rolling prairie lands, where the Missouri and Mississippi Basin tapers into the flats, while at the middle – encompassing all or parts of the provinces and states of Alberta, Saskatchewan, North and South Dakota, Wyoming, and Montana – are the true High Plains, an ancient domain of the buffalo. The region is criss-crossed by rivers such as the Powder, Bighorn and Platte, which produced lush valleys and islands of woodlands, so vital to the lifestyle of its nomadic human inhabitants – the Plains Indians.

On the Northern Plains, lived such tribes as the Blackfeet, Cree, and Assiniboin, on the Central Plains, the Sioux, Cheyenne, Arapaho, and Crow and on the Southern Plains, the Comanche, Kiowa, and Jicarilla Apache. To the west were the Shoshone, who shared a Plateau and Plains culture, and in the east, along the Missouri and Mississippi, were such groups as the Mandan, Hidatsa, Arikara, Pawnee, and Omaha – often referred to as the Prairie tribes. A variety of linguistic family stocks were represented in this region – Algonquian, Siouan, Caddoan, Uto-Aztecan, and Athapaskan – reflecting a diversity of earlier cultural backgrounds, which flavored their mythology. The purely nomadic tribes such as the Blackfeet, Sioux (Lakota), and Comanche were rich in horses and they roamed the Plains following the buffalo, living in tipis. Other tribes, such as the Mandan, Pawnee, and Omaha, lived in so-called earth lodges, only utilizing the tipi on hunting trips to the Plains. These people have been ranked as the richest Indians in America, wealth being based on the quantity of food available, such as buffalo meat, wild vegetables, and berries. In this society, men implored the spirits associated with both animals (see the Cheyenne myth of

Four masked spirit impersonators representing the four directions. These are probably Mescalero Apaches and photographed on the San Carlos Reservation in Arizona between 1898 and 1902. The distinctive costume of these so-called Gahan dancers included the black buckskin masks surmounted by carved and painted wooden slats. It is not unusual for them to carry bows and arrows (which two are doing here) – this suggests that part of the ritual was to do with the conferral of japane diyi or 'war medicine'.

the Buffalo Keepers, Chapter 6) and with the Sky of which the Sun was generally considered to be supreme, although the Morning and Evening Stars were particularly important to the Cheyenne (Chapter 3) and Pawnee (Chapter 6), respectively. All had a belief in a pervading force that could make man, animal or plant alive with power. Plains ceremonies were invariably described in terms of mythological tales. The myths also strongly related to the origin of Man and the earth, heroes and the topography. Thus, in the Blackfeet Genesis (Chapter 1), it is the mythical figure of Napi or 'Old Man' who not only created men and animals and laid out the land, but also demonstrated the power of dreams and taught the people many things. Thus, sacred myths served to express a fundamental pattern of conduct, which, to a limited extent, regimented the population. The myths were often dramatized in complex ceremonies and in consequence were basically unchanged through successive generations, examples being the Sioux Sun Dance and the Mandan O-kee-pa (both Chapter 6).

CALIFORNIA

To the west of the Great Basin, across the Sawtooth Mountains, lived a mixture of tribes in the region that is now California. Here, some five of the six language families in North America are represented. This contrasts markedly with such areas as the Northeast, where Algonquian and Muskogean speakers only are found. The probable explanation for this is that the country, being on the edge of the Pacific, afforded a stopping-off place for the many migrating groups, small detachments of which, possibly weary of the travel or just quarrelsome, settled here and there. These small groups – often referred to as 'tribelets' - exhibited a surprising hostility to one another, each developing very distinctive customs. In the north of the region were the Karok and Shasta, south of them were such tribes as the Pomo, Maidu and Chumash, noted for their coiled and twined basketry. The tribelets lived in small villages in dome-shaped brush huts or those made of a framework of poles covered with tule mats. They were semi-nomadic and there was considerable dependence on fish, though small animals – rabbits, birds, deer, and mountain sheep – were also hunted.

It is difficult to summarize the mythology of these very diverse groups. However, among the northern ones – such as the Karok and Shasta – there was a definite idea of a single creator who was sometimes aggravated by the Coyote Trickster. 'Old Man' or Chareya, as the creator, is the subject of the Shasta myth reproduced in Chapter 1; it contains several elements – creation of animals and the landscape, for example – which are fairly typical of this style of myth from Northern California.

THE NORTHWEST COAST

This is a very distinctive cultural area although there are considerable variations from north to south. The Northwest Coast culture extended from the Alaskan panhandle through coastal British Columbia and south to the Columbia River in Washington State. To the north were the so-called 'Maritime tribes', who lived mainly on the coastal islands of Alaska and British Columbia. They included such famous totem-pole carvers as the Haida, Nootka, Tlingit, and Tsimshian, while the River and Bay tribes occupied the mainland on the Pacific Coast – such groups as the Bella-Coola and Makah – while to their south and bordering Northern California were the Tillamook and Yurok, whose cultures merged with that of the Californian tribes.

What the buffalo was to the Plains people, so the salmon was to the Northwest Coast people – this magnificent fish, with its oily, rich meat, swam each summer up the numerous rivers from the Pacific. Additionally, there were bountiful supplies of deep-sea halibut and cod, shellfish and sea otter, sea-lion and whales – these last were hunted in dugout canoes by many of these coastal tribes.

These groups were also skilled in woodworking, the extensive, dense, almost impassable, forests providing cedar, redwood, and pine, most of which was relatively soft and straight grained. From such natural resources they built commodious houses, sea-going canoes and, most impressive of all in some of the northern villages, the totem-pole, whilst a magnificent, much coveted blanket was made by the Chilkats a band of Tlingits who lived in Southern Alaska.

Northwest Coast mythology is particularly rich and many of their origin stories begin with an account of some supreme power living in the skies, which was viewed as a multilayered domain where powerful beings, often in human form, dwelt. Thus, tales of monsters – first animal, then human – and cannibals who crushed men's skulls or witches who were associated with shamans' graves abound (see Chapter 2). Many myths centre around a Trickster – sometimes Raven, sometimes Robin, Blue Jay, or Mink. These were always clever creatures who taught mankind many things, for in this society humans were not considered to be superior to animals. Thus, in myths relating to the origin of the totem-pole (Chapter 2), it is Raven, not man, who is credited with bringing it to the Kwakiutl: this contrasts markedly with the known facts that extensive woodcarving was probably not practiced by the Northwest Coast tribes until iron tools were introduced in the late eighteenth century, mainly by Russian ships, trading in sea otter pelts, which were much coveted in the Orient.

Blackfeet man wearing willow sticks wrapped around his head, date not recorded but in the period 1900-20. This is obviously part of the Sun Dance ritual during which a hundred willow boughs were brought in by a Warrior Society and laid against the framework of the Sun Dance lodge.

THE NORTHEAST

This cultural area stretches west from the Atlantic coast to the northwestern shore of Lake Superior and then south to the Ohio and Cumberland Rivers extending to the North Carolina-Virginia coastal plain. To define the Indian cultures more precisely, this vast region is generally subdivided into three geographic areas – Great Lakes-Riverine, Saint Lawrence Lowlands, and Coastal. The major tribes associated with this region mainly belong to Algonquian and Iroquoian linguistic stock. In the northwest, centred around Lake Superior, were the Chippewa; to the south of this large tribe (some 25,000 in circa 1760) were the Menominee, Illinois, and Winnebago, this last actually being of a Siouan linguistic stock. To the north were the Abenaki, Maliseet-Passamaquoddy, and Micmac and to the south of them the Iroquois Confederacy, which consisted of six loosely united tribes – the Mohawk, Oneida, Onondaga, Cayuga, Seneca, and Tuscarora, who were often referred to as the 'People of the Longhouse' as they traditionally used dwellings, many up to 30 meters in length, which accommodated eight to ten families. House types and costume varied considerably; in addition to those who lived in longhouses, other families lived in birch or elm bark covered wigwams, but all wore soft-soled moccasins. Beautiful quillwork and moosehair embroidery – later beadwork – was made by many of these groups. Transportation depended firmly on the canoe and all used the snow-shoe. A crude type of pottery in addition to mats, textiles and bags, generally finely woven from cedar bark or nettle fibre, were produced throughout the area. Bags not infrequently displayed a Thunderbird and underwater monster motif on the front and back, referring to Sky and Under World powers,

A Zuni street probably at the Pueblo in New Mexico, photographed by J. K. Hillers in 1879, who gives the names of the people as In ih ti at the left and Ho ta at the right. Note the burros or donkeys, which were a common form of pack animal in the Pueblo region and, as can be seen here, were capable or transporting exceptionally large loads.

the inside of the bag symbolizing the Earth, which separated these two great powers. While diverse in many cultural traits, the area was actually united by several common cosmological beliefs, the most pronounced being a recognition of three great cosmic zones – the Under World, the Earth, and the Upper World of the sky and sun. These beliefs manifested themselves in the various ceremonies such as the Iroquois midwinter renewal ceremony, which they called the 'Dream Festival', where the 'Holder of the Heavens' was believed to have decreed that the ceremony should be performed on earth as it was carried out in the sky world. Associations of this sky world and their powers and gifts are the basis of the Passamaquoddy, Abenaki, Onondaga, and Chippewa myths reproduced in Chapters 2 and 3. Likewise, the power of the 'Giver of Life' as touched on by the Chippewa myths of the first man and woman and of the gifts of light, fire and water (Chapters 1 and 5) is echoed in the tribe's Midewinwin or 'Grand Medicine Society' ceremony. This was documented by a complex series of pictographs engraved on birch bark and emphasized the prolonging of life by right living as decreed by the Great Manitou, the staunch friend of man.

THE SUBARCTIC

The culture of the Subarctic area spans the whole continent of North America from Alaska east to the Labrador peninsula and dipping down below the Hudson Bay and Lake Winnipeg. When the first Europeans arrived in the mid-eighteenth century, the estimated population was no more than 60,000, the majority of whom were Athapaskan or Algonquian speaking peoples who occupied an estimated area of 5,000,000 sq km (approximately 2,000,000 sq miles).

The terrain in this vast region varies considerably from Arctic-alpine tundra in the north to open woodland tundra to the south, which in turn merges into boreal forests or parkland with a scattering of trees on a wide expanse of grassland. Much of the present provinces of the Yukon, Northwest Territories and northern parts of British Columbia, Alberta, Saskatchewan, Ontario, and Quebec and including the whole of Newfoundland, are encompassed in this Subarctic cultural area. The Athapaskan speaking tribes were such people as the Kutchin and Tanana in the Yukon, the Dogrib, Beaver, and Chipewyan in the Northwest Territories and northern parts of Alberta and Saskatchewan, while the Algonquians were various bands of Cree, Northern Ojibwa, Naskapi, and Montagnais – the latter two tribes occupying the northern part of Quebec and Labrador. Many of the groups consisted of extended nomadic family units and were somewhat isolated from one another since food resources were often scarce; caribou and moose were primarily hunted, but smaller game, such as hare, rabbit, and various waterfowl formed an important part of their diet, as did fish.

The Algonquian tribes tended to use the conical shaped wigwam, and the Athapaskans a dome shaped dwelling covered with birch bark or skins; in both cases the fireplace was in the center. Summers in this region are warm but of short duration, winters are harsh, bitterly cold and long. It was during these lengthy months of enforced inactivity that the story-tellers recounted the myths and legends of the tribes and the art of scapulimancy was practised. For the latter, large caribou or moose shoulder blade bones were held over a fire and the cracks and blackened spots were 'read' and fantastic stories related, all in direct proportion to the imagination of the narrator! Stories referring to cannibals, bushmen, and sky spirits and powers, abounded, these last illustrated by the Athapaskan Sun and Moon myth in Chapter 3, while the importance of wood for survival in this harsh land (for making implements, snow-shoes, fire-drills, weapons, and masks for ceremonial use) is touched on in a tale relating to the origin of pine (Chapter 2). Subarctic mythology tended to reflect the precariousness of human existence: it made repeated references to the unpredictable aspects of daily life so helping the listeners to find their place and establish correct behaviour patterns in a largely uncompromising, hostile environment.

THE ARCTIC

Frequently considered as one of the last, virtually untouched environments on earth, the Arctic region stretches almost 6500 km (about 4000 miles) from the coast of Greenland west to the coastline of Siberia. Here lived three separate groups, all derived from the Eskimo-Aleuts, who migrated across the Bering Strait from Siberia some 10,000 years ago – the most recent of the indigenous peoples of the North America whose language exhibits a high degree of distinctness from other languages either in the New World or Old. To the northwest lived the Aleut, occupying a string of islands, the Aleutian Islands, which stretched into the Bering Sea. The Yupik occupied both sides of the Bering Strait, while the Inuit-Inupiaq tribe extended from Greenland to Alaska and inhabited the whole of Arctic Canada.

The most widespread self designations for Eskimos-Aleutian speakers actually fall into several categories, some of which may be translated into 'real genuine person'. By the 1970s, however, because it was believed (erroneously) that Eskimo was a pejorative term, meaning 'eaters of raw meat', it was agreed, after considerable debate, that the term 'Inuit' would be adopted for all Eskimos, regardless of their local usages.

Although the Inuit have diverse cultures, common to all these people was the use of skin boats, harpoons, bladder or inflated skin floats, pronged bird spears, two winged salmon spears, lamps, stone pots, house platforms, tailored clothing, ivory carving, the use of a social house ('village hall'), and shamanistic types of myth or tale. The myth selected for this cultural area that relates to the Raven (Chapter 5) is from the Pacific Eskimo who occupied the mainland coast of Alaska and Kodiak Island. The settlements of these groups were generally limited to the fringes of the coast and because this area was largely free of ice, the main method of hunting was the sea mammal chase augmented by gathering and saltwater fishing. Their skin boats – kayaks – had a distinctive upturned bow, which perfectly suited the calm seas so characteristic of this region.

Mythological tales integrated a range of ceremonies, dances, rituals and feasts, and contact with the supernatural beings was achieved through the wearing of masks or in a trance. As with all Inuit groups, there were numerous taboos – often related in the myths – which were the very basis of religious life. These taboos were concerned with hunting activities, various game animals, and critical phases in a person's life cycle. In all this, the place of the shaman was paramount and they confounded the common man by use of a sacred or secret language in communicating with the spirit world. The higher powers were thus placated, as in the wise actions of the Chief on Kodiak Island, which are related in the myth of the Raven and which is discussed in more detail in the introduction to Chapter 5.

Mikasuki Seminole women using wooden mortar and pestles, photographed about 1890, probably near the Big Cypress Swamp, Florida. The mortar was hollowed out by charring the center of a wood log; the carved pestle was purposely left heavy above the handle to ensure efficient grinding of the hard, dried corn. The corn meal was used in a soup, together with the grated roots of the coontie plant (a wild cycad) making a soup called sofkie.

−1−

Creation Myths

I N SEVERAL NORTH AMERICAN INDIAN MYTHOLOGIES there is reference to the wind brooding over the primeval ocean in the form of a gigantic bird. The world is then created by various animals, who are called upon by the Creator to dive through the waters and bring up sufficient mud to form a beginning of the earth: some myths, such as that of the Muskogean (p. 26), extend to this mud being transformed into flesh and bone, whilst those tribes on the Plateau, such as the Shoshone and Bannock, refer to its use not only to make people but also the dome of the sky.

Bizarre reversals of events sometimes occur in these creation mythologies, thus the Algonquians relate that their great god, Michabo, was one day surprised to see animals entering a great lake and disappearing. He followed them into the waters with the object of rescuing them, but as he did so, the lake suddenly overflowed and submerged the entire earth. The great god then despatched a raven with directions to find a piece of earth that might serve as a nucleus for a new world, but the bird returned from its quest unsuccessful. Then the god sent an otter on a like errand, but it too failed to bring back the requisite terrestrial germ. At last a muskrat was sent on the same mission, and it returned with sufficient earth to enable Michabo to recreate the solid land. The trees had become denuded of their branches, so the god discharged arrows at them, which provided them with new boughs. After this, Michabo married the muskrat, and from their union sprang the human race. In the Blackfeet Genesis myth (p. 37). Michabo becomes Napi or 'Old Man', who formed the first humans from clay and then gave them plants, animals and showed them how to make bows and arrows. During the reservation period, when white people dominated and destroyed traditional Blackfeet culture, this myth was extended: the reason for this disaster, the Blackfeet said, was that they had failed to obey Napi's laws.

The emphasis on emergence from water is a recurring them, as exemplified by the Zuni creation myth (p. 31), where a green scum formed both Mother Earth and Father Sky, while the Apaches, an Athapaskan speaking people who migrated to the southwest at least 400 years ago, make reference to remnants of a primeval ocean (p. 33), perhaps an echo from the time when they lived adjacent to the Bering Sea in the far north of Canada. It is clear from the Choctaw creation story (p. 28; quoted from Swanton, 1931, pp. 202-4) that the Deluge figured prominently in their mythology. The Choctaw actually referred to this event as *Oka Falama*, 'the returned waters', which suggests that they believed 'water to have covered everything at the first creation' (Swanton, 1931, p. 202).

Reference to the emergence of humans from under the earth is also a widespread creation myth, one version of which is reproduced in the Mandan creation myth (p. 26). Variants of this theme have been identified from such widely spaced groups as the Choctaws and Creeks in the Southeast to the Haida, Tsimshian, Kwakiutl, and Tlingit on the Northwest Coast, while in the Southwest, the Zuni creation myth refers to the tribe travelling through four underground caves, finally emerging to the Upper World of Seeing and Knowledge.

In contrast, a Shasta (California) creation myth (p. 45) emphasizes sky powers: Chareya or 'Old Man Above' bores a hole in the sky through which he climbed through to the earth, where he created the trees and animals. In this respect it resembles the Pawnee (Plains) myths, which refer to Tirawahat or 'The One Above'. Tirawahat was said to be the maker of all things and it was he who decreed a marriage between the Evening and Morning Stars, whose offspring subsequently populated the earth.

It has been observed that the Muskogean myth (p. 26) closely resembles the story in the Book of Genesis: in both man is made from mud, while in the former the pigeons or doves appear analogous to the brooding creative Spirit. Hardin suggests that the parallels are so striking that one is almost 'forced to conclude that this is one of the instances in which Gospel conceptions have been engrafted on a native legend' (Hardin, ed., p. 3). However, before attributing such similarities to the teaching of Christian missionaries, consideration should be given to the fact that when comparisons are made between the various American Indian myths and legends and their pre-Columbian models, a more reasonable conclusion is that the Bible is but one expression of the beliefs common to humanity 'which developed in their own way in the New World' (Brotherston, p. 153).

However, not all creation myths follow this pattern: thus, the Abenaki of the Northeastern Woodlands claimed that they were created by the all-powerful sun, which first formed the universe and then fertilized the earth and with its

PREVIOUS PAGE An Apache woman hauling firewood on her back, date not recorded but probably 1900-20. The so-called hogan (from the Navajo, goghan 'house') is a typical Apache dwelling and consisted of a framework of poles, bent together at the top and covered with brush, bark or skins. Note the large water jugs on the ground; these were often made of basketry and waterproofed by use of pinon pitch.

penetrating rays brought forth living creatures. In the Chippewas it was the 'Great Manitou' (Hardin, ed., p. 126) in the form of an enormous bird, from whose egg a man emerged.

Whatever the versions of these creation myths, there was a widespread belief that they were the most sacred, and there is some evidence that traditional religious leaders were opposed to them being fully recorded. As with all mankind, North American Indian creation myths, with great ingenuity and creativity, attempted to answer the questions as to where everything came from; the 'how' and the 'why' of the often paradoxical world about them.

Nijogijig, *a Chippewa man of the Red Lake Band, Minnesota. The spiritual life of the Chippewa Indians were centered around the Grand Medicine Lodge or Midewiwin ceremonies, whose main aims were healing and the teaching of good ethical conduct. Note the bird's head – probably a kingfisher – attached to the stem and representative of animal powers: the creation myth related here refers to man emerging from a bird's egg.*

STORY OF THE FIRST MAN AND WOMAN
(*Chippewa*)

The Great Manitou had his home in the Land of Peace. Before he became a man and his face was cut in the stone, he was a great bird and his nest was in the pipestone rocks.

He fed on the wild buffaloes that lived on the prairies. He could carry two buffaloes in his claws, he always ate them near his nest; this is why the rocks are red.

The tracks of the manitou bird can be seen near the Land of Peace. The Indians know where to find these tracks and will show them to the white man.

Seminole women, the Cow Creek Reservation in Florida, photographed about 1917. These people were of a Muskogean linguistic group and emerged as 'Seminoles' circa 1775, formerly being classed as 'Lower Creeks' following the destruction of the towns of their kinsmen, the Apalachee, by the English in the early 1700s. Muskogean creation mythology, however, relates that the people were moulded from the mud that began the earth.

The Great Serpent is older than mankind. He was alive before the first man was made. He found the nest of the manitou bird; there was one egg in the nest. The manitou heard the egg move. He was miles away, but he flew with a great rock in his claws and killed the serpent. The rock broke open the egg, and out of it came a grown man, but the rock lay upon his feet and he could not walk. He had to stand in one place, for the manitou bird would not set him free until he knew many things.

The man learned how to hunt the buffalo, for he could see many miles. He learned how to tan and use the buffalo skin, he learned the language of birds; they would come when he would call their names, he learned how to make and use the bow and arrow.

The manitou bird covered the man with a great buffalo skin, but his head was not covered, for he had much black hair. The first man was slow to learn and he stood many moons in his place in the pipestone rocks: nothing came to hurt him.

When he had learned much, he woke one morning and found a woman standing beside him. The manitou bird pulled away the stone from the feet of the man. He shook his wings and the man and woman ran to the prairie.

These two were the first of all people. They were Indians. All mankind know they were the first to live on the earth.

THE MUSKOGEAN CREATION STORY
(*Muskogee*)

The Muskogean Indians believe that in the beginning the primeval waste of waters alone was visible. Over the dreary expanse two pigeons or doves flew hither and thither, and in course of time observed a single blade of grass spring above the surface. The solid earth followed gradually, and the terrestrial sphere took its present shape. A great hill, Nunne Chaha, rose and the midst and in the center of this was the house of the deity Esaugetuh Emissee the "Master of Breath." He took the clay which surrounded his abode, and from it molded the first men, and as the waters still covered the earth he was compelled to build a great wall upon which to dry the folk he had made. Gradually the soft mud became transformed into bone and flesh, and Esaugetuh was successful in directing the waters into their proper channels, reserving the dry land for the men he had created.

ORIGIN OF THE MANDAN
(*Mandan*)

The Mandan tribes of the Sioux suppose that their nation lived in a subterranean village near a vast lake. Clambering up the roots of a great grape-vine that penetrated from the earth above, several of them got a sight of the upper world, which they found to be rich and well stocked with both animal and vegetable food. Those of them who had seen the new-found world above returned to their home bringing such glowing accounts of its wealth and pleasantness that the others resolved to forsake their dreary underground dwelling for the delights of the sunny sphere above. The entire population set out, and started to climb up the roots of the vine, but not more than half the tribe had ascended when the plant broke owing to the weight of a corpulent woman. The Mandans imagine that after death they will return to the underground world in which they originally dwelt, the worthy reaching the village by way of the lake, the bad having to abandon the passage by reason of the weight of their sins.

The Minnetarees believed that their original ancestor emerged from the waters of a lake bearing in his hand an ear of corn, and the Mandans possessed a myth very similar to that of the Muskogees concerning their origin.

The Mandan chief, Rushing War Eagle, son of Four Bears, photographed in Washington, D.C., probably in 1874. A much respected chief, he was the sole survivor of the 1837 smallpox epidemic that killed his parents. Rushing War Eagle wears a fine bear claw necklace and carries a long stemmed pipe with a head of carved red catlinite stone.

LEFT *A Choctaw ball game, photographed near Philadelphia (Mississippi) in 1925. This was a popular game among the Choctaw, the goal posts, which the ball must touch, being some 65 meters or so apart. Even during the game, the 'conjurers were conspicuous', they 'ran up to the posts, battering them with their ball sticks'. This they did 'to scare the spirit of bad luck away' (Swanton, 1931, p. 150).*

CHOCTAW CREATION MYTH
(*Choctaw*)

In ancient times, after many generations of mankind had lived and passed from the stage of being, the race became so corrupt and wicked – brother fighting against brother and wars deluging the earth with human blood and carnage – that the Great Spirit became greatly displeased and finally determined to destroy the human race; therefore he sent a great prophet to them who proclaimed from tribe to tribe, and from village to village, the fearful tidings that the human race was soon to be destroyed. None believed his words, and they lived on in their wickedness as if they did not care, and the seasons came again and went. Then came the autumn of the year, followed by many succeeding cloudy days and nights, during which the sun by day and the moon and stars by night were concealed from the earth; then succeeded a total darkness, and the sun seemed to have been blotted out; while darkness and silence with a cold atmosphere took possession of the earth. Mankind, wearied and perplexed, but not repenting or reforming, slept in darkness but to awake in darkness; then the mutterings of distant thunder began to be heard, gradually becoming incessant, until it reverberated in all parts of the sky and seemed to echo back even from the deep center of the earth. Then fear and consternation seized upon every heart and all believed the sun would never return. The Magi of the Choctaws spoke despondently in reply to the many interrogations of the alarmed people, and sang their death-songs which were but faintly heard in the mingled confusion that arose amid the gloom of the night that seemed would have no returning morn. Mankind went from place to place only by torch-light; their food stored away became mouldy and unfit for use; the wild animals of the forests gathered around their fires bewildered and even entered their towns and villages, seeming to have lost all fear of man. Suddenly a fearful crash of thunder, louder than ever before heard, seemed to shake the earth, and immediately after a light was seen glimmering seemingly far away to the North. It was soon discovered not to be the light of the returning sun, but the gleam of great waters advancing in mighty billows, wave succeeding wave as they rolled onward over the earth destroying everything in their path.

Then the wailing cry was heard coming from all directions. *Oka Falama, Oka Falama* "The returned waters." Stretching from horizon to horizon, it came pouring its massive waters onward. The foundations of the Great Deep were broken up. Soon the earth was entirely overwhelmed by the mighty and irresistible rush of the waters which swept away the human race and all animals, leaving the earth a desolate waste. Of all mankind only one was saved, and that one was the mysterious prophet who had been sent by the Great

BELOW *Choctaw woman pounding corn, circa 1900. Although the pestle is traditional, the mortar is usually an upright hollowed log instead of a horizontal log as shown here. Although by 1885 there were overwhelming numbers of intruders in Choctaw territory they tended to resist social contact and continued to practice many of their traditional customs and eat traditional food.*

Spirit to warn the human race of their near approaching doom. This prophet saved himself by making a raft of sassafras logs by the direction of the Great Spirit, upon which he floated upon the great waters that covered the earth, as various kinds of fish swam around him, and twined among the branches of the submerged trees, while upon the face of the waters he looked upon the dead bodies of men and beasts, as they rose and fell upon the heaving billows.

After many weeks floating he knew not where, a large black bird came to the raft flying in circles above his head. He called to it for assistance, but it only replied in loud, croaking tones, then flew away and was seen no more. A few days after, a bird of bluish colour, with red eyes and beak, came and hovered over the raft, to which the prophet spoke and asked if there were a spot of dry land anywhere to be seen in the wide waste of waters. Then it flew around his head a few moments fluttering its wings and uttering a mournful cry, then flew away in the direction of that part of the sky where the new sun seemed to be sinking into the rolling waves of the great ocean of waters. Immediately a strong wind sprang up and bore the raft rapidly in that direction. Soon night came on, and the moon and stars again made their appearance, and the next morning the sun arose in its former splendor. Looking around, the prophet saw an island in the distance, toward which the raft was slowly drifting, and before the sun had gone down seemingly again into the world of waters, the raft had touched the island, upon which he landed and encamped, and being wearied and lonely he soon forgot his anxieties in sleep. When morning came, looking around the island, he found it covered with all varieties of animals – excepting the mammoth which had been destroyed. He also found birds and fowls of every kind in vast numbers upon the island, among which he discovered the identical black bird which had visited him upon the waters, and then left him to his fate: and, as he regarded it as a cruel bird, he named it Fulushto (Raven) – a bird of ill omen to the ancient Choctaws.

With great joy he also discovered the bluish bird which had caused the wind to blow his raft upon the island, and because of this act of kindness and its great beauty he called it Puchi Yushubah (Lost Pigeon: "pǎchi yoshoba" the turtle dove).

After many days the waters passed away; and in the course of time Puchi Yushubah became a beautiful woman, whom the prophet soon after married, and by them the world was again peopled.

LEFT Toshkachito, *known to whites as Joe Silestine, a Choctaw photographed at Bayou Lacombe, Louisiana in 1909. This man is demonstrating the use of a cane hunting blow gun, which generally extended up to three meters or more in length and fired darts of sharp pointed sticks that could kill small animals and birds up to eight meters away. The Choctaw were an important tribe of the Muskogean linguistic stock, and their name possibly derives from the Spanish* chato, *which means 'flat' or 'flattened' and refers to the early custom of flattening the head.*

ZUNI CREATION MYTH
(*Zuni*)

Awonawilona, the creator, fertilized the sea with his own flesh and hatched it with his own heat. From
this, green scums were formed, which became the fourfold mother Earth and the all-covering father
Sky, from whom sprang all creatures. Then from the nethermost of the four caves of the world the seed of
men and the creatures took form and grew; just as with eggs in warm places worms quickly form and appear,
and, growing, soon burst their shells to produce birds, tadpoles, or serpents, so man and all the creatures
multiplied in many kinds. Thus did the lowermost world-cave become overfilled with living things, full of
unfinished creatures, which, crawled like reptiles in the darkness, thickly crowding together and treading on
each other, with one spitting on another or doing some other indecency. In this manner the murmurings and
lamentations became loud, and many amidst the growing confusion sought to escape, growing wiser and
more manlike. Then Po-shai-an-K'ia, the foremost and wisest of men, arising from the nethermost sea, came

ABOVE *Harvest Dance of the Zuni, photographed by J. K. Hillers about 1879. Note the large structure in the right background, which is the remains of an old Spanish Mission built at the end of the seventeenth century. In 1680 the Zuni revolted against the missionaries, sickened by the progressive destruction of their mythology and religion by Christian influences.*

among the men and living things. Pitying them, he found a way out of that first world-cave yet through such a dark and narrow path that some, though seeing somewhat, crowded after him but could not follow, so eagerly did they struggle with one another. Alone then did Po-shai-an-K'ia come from one cave to another into this world which was then like an island, lying amidst the vast, wet and unstable world-waters. He sought and found the Sun-Father and besought him to deliver the men and creatures from that nethermost world.

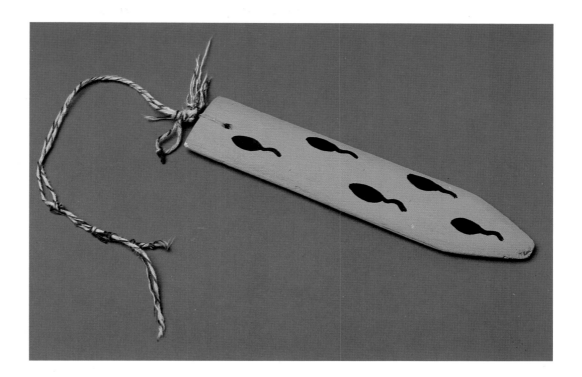

ABOVE RIGHT *A Southwestern bull-roarer used in dances to frighten away the evil spirits. When spun in the air by its string, it made a loud buzzing noise. Note the tadpoles, a widely used motif which often referred to life emerging from a primordial lake. In the Zuni creation myth they are described as bursting and emerging into life.*

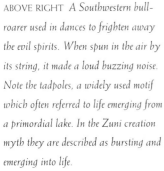

APACHE CREATION MYTH
(*Apache*)

In the underworld, Un-gó-ya-yĕn-ni, there was no sun, moon, or light of any kind, except that emanating from large eagle feathers which the people carried about with them. This method of lighting proved unsatisfactory, and the head men of the tribe gathered in council to devise some plan for lighting the world more brightly. One of the chiefs suggested that they make a sun and a moon. A great disk of yellow paint was made upon the ground, and then placed in the sky. Although this miniature creation was too small to give much light, it was allowed to make one circuit of the heavens before it was taken down and made larger. Four times the sun set and rose, and four times it was enlarged, before it was "as large as the earth and gave plenty of light." In the underworld dwelt a wizard and a witch, who were much incensed at man's presumption, and made such attempts to destroy the new luminaries that both the sun and the moon fled from the lower world, leaving it again in darkness, and made their escape to this earth, where they have never been molested, so that, until the present time, they continue to shine by night and by day. The loss of the sun and moon brought the people together, that they might take council concerning the means of restoring the lost light. Long they danced and sang, and made medicine. At length it was decided that they should go in search of the sun. The Indian medicine-men caused four mountains to spring up, which grew by night with great noise, and rested by day. The mountains increased in size until the fourth night, when they nearly reached the sky. Four boys were sent to seek the cause of the failure of the mountains to reach the opening in the sky, ba-ná-za-ä, through which the sun and moon had disappeared. The boys followed the tracks of two girls who had caused the mountains to stop growing, until they reached some burrows in the side of the mountain, where all trace of the two females disappeared. When their story was told to the people, the medicine-men said, "You who have injured us shall be transformed into rabbits, that you may be of some use to mankind; your bodies shall be eaten," and the rabbit has been used for food by the human race down to the present day.

RIGHT *A Western Apache woman of Arizona (Fort Apache Reservation) carrying a baby in a cradle board on her back, circa 1907. Note that the woman's hair is unusually short, suggesting that a few months before this photograph was taken, it was cut to commemorate the death of a close relative. The typical child's cradle is made from a series of wooden slats that support the infant and cross the vertical frame, while the face guard is of a series of horizontal willow withes.*

LEFT *Two Apache hunters. The man on the left is Chato, a Chiricahua warrior of high rank and a close associate of Geronimo. Note his knitted socks, which were probably an army issue. They both wear typical Apache costume of the period, headbands, high moccasins (on right-hand figure) and long breechclouts. Their weapons are the usual Apache flat bow with long arrows.*

All then journeyed to the tops of the mountains, where a ladder was built which reached the aperture in the sky or roof of the underworld. The badger was then sent out to explore the earth above; the messenger soon returned, and reported water everywhere except around the margin of the opening. The legs of the badger were covered with mud, which accounts for their dark color at the present day. Four days later, the turkey was sent to see if the waters had subsided. The turkey reported no land yet to be seen above. As the turkey came in contact with the foam of the flood surrounding the opening his tail became wet and heavy; in shaking this he scattered filmy drops upon his wings, and that is why the feathers of the turkey to the present day present an iridescent play of colors. Then the Wind came to the anxious people and said, "If you will ask me to help you, I will drive back the water for you." Thus the first prayers came to be addressed to the Wind, which yet remains a powerful deity. When the Wind had rolled back the waters to the limits of the present ocean, the Indians began to ascent the ladder; four times the ladder broke with them, and four times it was replaced by a new one. All the people reached the new world except one old woman, too old and infirm to climb the ladder, who said to them: "I do not wish to leave the land of my youth. Go your way and leave me here; you will come back to join me when you die. You have forgotten one thing; you will soon discover what it is." For four days after their emergence no one could sleep; then the people remembered the warning of the old woman, and two boys were sent down to the underworld to learn what it was that had been forgotten. The old woman said in reply to their question, "You forgot to take lice with you, without them you cannot sleep." She took two black ones from her hair and two white ones from her body, saying, "These will be all you will need, for they will increase night and day." So it has happened that the Apaches sleep well to this day because they harbor these parasites upon their bodies.

Coyotero Apache group in a brush shelter. Date not recorded by prior to 1907. The Apache were a nomadic people subsisting mainly on the products of the chase and wild berries and roots. Dwellings were, as shown here, brush shelters, which were easily erected and well adapted to the environment and constant shifting.

So well had the Wind performed his task of drying up the waters, that none remained for the people to drink; but prayers addressed to the deity were answered by the appearance of the present springs and rivers. The few lakes that occur in the Apache country are remnants of the primeval ocean. All the inhabitants of the earth were then Apaches, but the Cheyennes and Utes were soon created from willows. The supreme God Yi-ná-yĕs-gŏ-i, directed the people westward; as they journeyed, small parties became separated, and settled by the wayside. These were given different names and languages.

THE BLACKFEET GENESIS
(Blackfeet)

All animals of the Plains at one time heard and knew him, and all birds of the air heard and knew him. All things that he had made understood him, when he spoke to them-the birds, the animals, the people.

Old Man was traveling about, south of here, making the people. He came from the south, traveling north, making animals and birds as he passed along. He made the mountains, prairies, timber, and brush first. So he went along, traveling northward, making things as he went, putting rivers here and there, and falls on them, putting red paint here and there in the ground,-fixing up the world as we see it today. He made the Milk River (the Teton) and crossed it, and, being tired, went up on a little hill and lay down to rest. As he lay on his back, stretched out on the ground, with arms extended, he marked himself out with stones – the shape of his body, head, legs, arms, and everything. There you can see those rocks today. After he had rested, he went on northward, and stumbled over a knoll and fell down on his knees. Then he said, "You are a bad thing to be stumbling against;" so he raised up two large buttes there, and named them the Knees and they are so called to this day. He went on further north, and with some of the rocks he carried with him he built the Sweet Grass Hills.

Old Man covered the plains with grass for the animals to feed on. He marked off a piece of ground, and in it he made all kinds of roots and berries grow – camas, wild carrots, wild turnips, sweet-root, bitter-root, sarvis berries, bull berries, cherries, plums, and rosebuds. He put trees in the ground. He put all kinds of animals on the ground. When he made the bighorn with its big head and horns, he made it out on the prairie. It did not seem to travel easily on the prairie: it was awkward and could not go fast. So he took it by one of its horns, and led it up into the mountains and turned it loose: and it skipped about among the rocks, and went up fearful places with ease. So he said, "This is the place that suits you: this is what you are fitted for, the rocks and the mountains." While he was in the mountains, he made the antelope out of dirt, and turned it loose, to see how it would go. It ran so fast that it fell over some rocks and hurt itself. He saw that this would not do, and took the antelope down on the prairie, and turned it loose; and it ran away fast and gracefully, and he said, "This is what you are suited to."

One day Old Man determined that he would make a woman and a child; so he formed them both – the woman and the child, her son – of clay. After he had molded the clay in human shape, he said to the clay, "You must be people," and then he covered it up and left it, and went away. The next morning he went to the place and took the covering off, and saw that the clay shapes had changed a little. The second morning there was still more change, and the third still more. The fourth morning he went to the place, took the covering off, looked at the images and told them to rise and walk, and they did so. They walked down to the river with their Maker, and then he told them that his name was Na'pi, Old Man.

As they were standing by the river, the woman said to him, "How is it? Will we always live? Will there be no end to it?" He said: "I have never thought of that. We will have to decide it. I will take this buffalo chip and throw it in the river. If it floats, when people die, in four days they will become alive again, they will die for only four days. But if it sinks, there will be an end to them." He threw the chip into the river, and

OPPOSITE *An Apache woman of Arizona carrying a burden basket from her head, probably about 1900. The Apache were well known for their high skill in making baskets of the type shown here. She wears a fine fringed and beaded buckskin poncho of the type that was traditionally provided during a puberty ceremony — a ceremony that promoted longevity, physical strength, and good temperament.*

BELOW *View of the Blackfeet camp, photograph taken in 1915 probably near Browning, Montana. Left to right are Bill Shoot, Black Bull, Eagle Child, Stabs by Mistake, and Mrs. Brocky. To the right is a large medicine bundle supported on a tripod; such bundles — this is probably a so-called Beaver Bundle — were replete with mythological lore.*

it floated. The woman turned and picked up a stone, and said: "No, I will throw this stone in the river, if it floats we will always live, if it sinks people must die, that they may always be sorry for each other." The woman threw the stone into the water, and it sank. "There," said Old Man, "you have chosen. There will be an end to them."

It was not many nights after that the woman's child died, and she cried a great deal for it. She said to Old Man: "Let us change this. The law that you first made, let that be a law." He said: "Not so. What is made law must be law. We will undo nothing that we have done. The child is dead, but it cannot be changed. People will have to die."

That is how we came to be people. It is he who made us.

The first people were poor and naked, and did not know how to get a living. Old Man showed them the roots and berries, and told them that they could eat them; that in a certain month of the year they could peel the bark off some trees and eat it, that it was good. He told the people that the animals should be their food, and gave them to the people, saying, "There are your herds." He said: "All these little animals that live in the ground – rats, squirrels, skunks, beavers – are good to eat. You need not fear to eat of their flesh." He made all the birds that fly, and told the people that there was no harm in their flesh, that it could be eaten. The first people that he created he used to take about through the timber and swamps and over the prairies, and show them the different plants. Of a certain plant he would say, "The root of this plant, if gathered in a certain month of the year, is good for a certain sickness." So they learned the power of all herbs.

Blackfeet women cooking meat, photographed by Edward S. Curtis prior to 1927. Here, a tripod on which the cut meat is hung, supports a metal trade pot over a fire. The woman in the foreground wears a beautiful dress embellished with elk teeth. Prior to the introduction of pots, meat was cooked by 'stone boiling' – hot stones were dropped into a hide-lined hole so that the water boiled.

In those days there were buffalo. Now the people had not arms, but those black animals with long beards were armed; and once, as the people were moving about, the buffalo saw them, and ran after them, and hooked them, and killed and ate them. One day, as the Maker of the people was traveling over the country, he saw some of his children, that he had made, lying dead, torn to pieces and partly eaten by the buffalo. When he saw this he was very sad. He said: "This will not do. I will change this. The people shall eat the buffalo."

He went to some of the people who were left, and said to them, "How is it that you people do nothing to these animals that are killing you." The people said: "What can we do? We have no way to kill these animals, while they are armed and can kill us." Then said the Maker: "That is not hard. I will make you a weapon that will kill these animals." So he went out, and cut some sarvis berry shoots, and brought them in, and peeled the bark off them. He took a larger piece of wood, and flattened it, and tied a string to it, and made a bow. Now, as he was the master of all birds and could do with them as he wished, he went out and caught one, and took feathers from its wing, and split them, and tied them to the shaft of wood. He tied feathers from its wing, and split them, and tied them to the shaft of wood. He tied four feathers along the shaft, and tried the arrow at a mark, and found that it did not fly well. He took these feathers off, and put on three; and when he tried it again, he found that it was good. He went out and began to break sharp pieces off the stones. He tried them, and found that the black flint stones made the test arrow points, and some white flints. Then he taught the people how to use these things.

Then he said: "The next time you go out, take these things with you, and use them as I tell you, and do not run from these animals. When they run at you, as soon as they get pretty close, shoot the arrows at them, as I have taught you; and you will see that they will run from you or will run in a circle around you."

Now, as people became plenty, one day three men went out on to the plain to see the buffalo, but they had no arms. They saw the animals, but when the buffalo saw the men, they ran after them and killed two of them, but one got away. One day after this, the people went on a little hill to look about, and the

Dried maize and cakes of pounded chokecherries in rawhide 'mortar'. The pounder is of Sioux make, the stone head is attached by rawhide and the handle decorated with white, green, yellow, and red seed beads. Wild berries and fruits were widely used and in the Blackfeet genesis, it was Napi or 'Old Man' who showed the people the use of fruits and berries.

buffalo saw them, and said, "Saiyah, there is some more of our food," and they rushed on them. This time the people did not run. They began to shoot at the buffalo with the bows and arrows Na'pi had given them, and the buffalo began to fall; but in the fight a person was killed.

At this time these people had flint knives given them, and they cut up the bodies of the dead buffalo. It is not healthful to eat the meat raw, so Old Man gathered soft dry rotten driftwood and made punk of it, and then got a piece of hard wood, and drilled a hole in it with an arrow point, and gave them a pointed piece of hard wood, and drilled a hole in it with an arrow point, and gave them a pointed piece of hard wood, and taught them how to make a fire with fire sticks, and to cook the flesh of these animals and eat it.

They got a kind of stone that was in the land, and then took another harder stone and worked one upon the other, and hollowed out the softer one, and made a kettle of it. This was the fashion of their dishes.

Also Old Man said to the people: "Now, if you are overcome, you may go and sleep, and get power. Something will come to you in your dream, that will help you. Whatever these animals tell you to do, you must obey them, as they appear to you in your sleep. Be guided by them. If anybody wants help, if you are alone and traveling, and cry aloud for help, your prayer will be answered. It may be by the eagles, perhaps by the buffalo or by the bears. Whatever animal answers your prayer, you must listen to him."

That was how the first people got through the world, by the power of their dreams.

After this, Old Man kept on traveling north. Many of the animals that he had made followed him as he went. The animals understood him when he spoke to them, and he used them as this servants. When he got to the north point of the Porcupine Mountains, there he made some more mud images of people, and blew breath upon them, and they became people. He made men and women. They asked him, What are we to eat?" He made many images of clay in the form of buffalo. Then he blew breath on these, and they stood up: and when he made signs to them, they started to run. Then he said to the people, "Those are your food." They said to him, "Well, now, we have those animals; how are we to kill them?" "I will show you," he said. He took them to the cliff, and made them build rock piles; and he made the people hide behind these piles of rock, and said, "When I lead the buffalo this way, as I bring them opposite to you rise up."

After he had told them how to act, he started on toward a herd of buffalo. He began to call them, and the buffalo started to run toward him, and they followed him until they were inside the line. Then he dropped back; and as the people rose up, the buffalo ran in a straight line and jumped over the cliff. He told the people to go and take the flesh of those animals. They tried to tear the limbs apart, but they could not. They tried to bite pieces out, and could not. So Old Man went to the edge of the cliff, and broke some pieces of stone with sharp edges, and told them to cut the flesh with these. When they had taken the skins from these animals, they set up some poles and put the hides on them, and so made a shelter to sleep under. There were some of these buffalo that went over the cliff that were not dead. Their legs were broken, but they were still alive. The people cut strips of green hide and tied stones in the middle, and made large mauls and broke in the skulls of the buffalo, and killed them.

After he had taught those people these things, he started off again, traveling north, until he came to where Bow and Elbow rivers meet. There he made some more people, and taught them the same things. From here he again went on northward. When he had come nearly to the Red Deer's River, he reached the hill where the Old Man sleeps. There he lay down and rested himself. The form of his body is to be seen there yet.

When he awoke from his sleep, he traveled further northward and came to a fine high hill. He climbed to the top of it, and there sat down to rest. He looked over the country below him, and it pleased him. Before him the hill was steep, and he said to himself, "Well, this is a fine place for sliding; I will have some fun," and he began to slide down the hill. The marks where he slid down are to be seen yet, and the place is known to all people as the "Old Man's Sliding Ground."

This is as far as the Blackfeet followed Old Man. The Crees know what he did further north.

In later times once, Na'pi said, "Here I will mark you off a piece of ground," and he did so. Then he said: "There is your land, and it is full of all kinds of animals, and many things grow in this land. Let no other

people come into it. This is for you five tribes (Blackfeet, Bloods, Piegans, Gros Ventres, Sarcees). When people come to cross the line, take your bows and arrows, your lances and your battle axes, and give them battle and keep them out. If they gain a footing, trouble will come to you."

Our forefathers gave battle to all people who came to cross these lines, and kept them out. Of late years we have let our friends, the white people, come in, and you know the result. We, his children, have failed to obey laws.

Running Owl's family (Blackfeet), photograph by Edward S. Curtis prior to 1910. This is obviously taken inside a tipi – note the geometrically decorated lining in the background. The women to the left and right are wearing dresses embellished with basket beads or pony beads while the child at the center is wearing a costume decorated with elk teeth.

The Blackfeet (Piegan) warrior, Lazy Boy, photographed by Donald Schmidt in Montana in 1947. At that time Lazy Boy was probably the oldest living Indian on the Reservation, having been born in 1855. Lazy Boy acted as an important informant on the use of the horse in Blackfeet Indian culture to the ethnologist, J. C. Ewers, who was present when this photograph was taken. Much Blackfeet mythology credits the first horses as being a gift from the sky or underwater spirits.

Grizzly bear claw talisman embellished with brass studs and hung with ribbons, used in the Chippewa Midewiwin or Grand Medicine Lodge Ceremonies. The power of the bear was widely recognized throughout the North American cultural areas, and a Shasta myth relates that the bear was 'Master of all'.

HOW OLD MAN ABOVE CREATED THE WORLD
(*Shasta*)

Long, long ago, when the world was so new that even the stars were dark, it was very, very flat. Chareya, Old Man Above, could not see through the dark to the new flat earth. Neither could he step down to it because it was so far below him. With a large stone he bored a hole in the sky. Then through the hole, he pushed down masses of ice and snow, until a great pyramid rose from the plain. Old Man Above climbed down through the hole he had made in the sky, stepping from cloud to cloud , until he could put his foot on top the mass of ice and snow. Then with one long step he reached the earth.

The sun shone through the hole in the sky and began to melt the ice and snow. It made holes in the ice and snow. When it was soft, Chareya bored with his finger into the earth, here and there, and planted the first trees. Streams from the melting snow watered the new trees and made them grow. Then he gathered the leaves which fell from the trees and blew upon them. They became birds. He took a stick and broke it into pieces. Out of the small end he made fishes and placed them in the mountain streams. Of the middle of the stick he made all the animals except the grizzly bear. From the big end of the stick came the grizzly bear, who was made master of all. Grizzly was large and strong and cunning. When the earth was new he walked upon two feet and carried a large club. So strong was Grizzly that Old Man Above feared the creature he had made. Therefore, so that he might be safe, Chareya hollowed out the pyramid of ice and snow as a tipi. There he lived for thousands of snows. The Indians knew he lived there because they could see the smoke curling from the smoke hole in his tipi. When the pale-face came, Old Man Above went away. There is no longer any smoke from the smoke hole. White men call the tipi Mount Shasta.

−2−

Origin Myths

I N ANY TRADITION, perhaps the function of myths most apparent to the outside observer is one of *explanation*. In this respect, the rich mythological tales associated with the various cultural areas of North America are no exception. Although the origin of such common occurrences as fire, thunder (p. 53) and witchcraft are repeated in various forms throughout the entire continent. Some – like the origins of wampum (p. 71), pipestone (p. 71; quoted from Ewers, ed., caption for Pl. 3') – or the first totem pole (p. 67) – relate to particular cultural areas.

There are several Iroquois legends of the Northeast that emphasize the traditional tribal diet of corn (p. 66), squash and bean crops. Often referred to as 'The Three Sisters', these were also called in Seneca, *De-o-ha-ko*, 'Our Life' or 'Our Supporters', while the Onondaga called them *Tune-ha-kwe*, 'Those we live on'. In one story, the Great Spirit gives corn to the Mohawks, squashes to the Onondagas and beans to the Senecas, thus dividing the three among the three Elder Brothers of the Iroquois confederacy. The foliage and flowers of these vital plants were said to represent their dresses, while benevolent spirits were said to not only protect the harvest from such blights as insects and mildew, but also to turn the squashes towards the sun to hasten their ripening.

Comparable legends occur in the Pueblos of the Southwest. In this desert climate, the cultivation of bountiful crops of maize, squashes, and beans was vital for survival in a region distinguished by a scarcity of game, wild fruit, and, above all, water. Thus, to obtain this last precious resource, the Hopi developed complex ceremonies with the Kachina gods who brought the moisture of the spirit world with them, nurturing the crops. Corn in particular, which originated in Mexico more than 7,000 years ago, was almost universally said to have its origins through a fertile corn mother or maiden and it was the woman in the Northeast who not only planted the seeds but also harvested the crop. In contrast, the men in the Pueblos planted the corn but again women were associated with its fertility, a female corn spirit being linked with each of the several different colours the ears took as they ripened.

As corn was to the physical well being, so tobacco was to the spirit of many North American tribes and was ceremonially utilized in all cultural areas, although the emphasis was somewhat reduced on the Northwest coast. Communication with the higher powers was through the rising smoke and seldom did a ceremony commence, a hunting or war party set forth, or a crop get planted, without the ritual use of tobacco; dried and crumbled, it was scattered in holy places, sprinkled on an open fire or smoked in pipes of reeds, wood, or stone. Its origin was explained by the tribes of the Northeast as a gift from the Great Spirit so that human beings could offer something of value to the higher powers. On the Plains, the Crow regarded the tobacco plant as the first to appear on earth, its origin being in the stars, and complex ceremonies of the Crow Tobacco Society – performed so that the needs of the people should be met – used tobacco seeds that had been specially selected for the star-like symbols sometimes found on them.

The pipe – usually with a stone bowl and wooden stem, although there were considerable variants throughout the cultural areas – was no less sacred than the tobacco smoked in it[1] Some of the finest pipes originated with the Sioux, the bowls being made of a soft red stone now called catlinite.[2] A Sioux legend (p. 71) relates that the stone was a gift from the Great Spirit, while the pipe itself was brought to the tribe by the White Buffalo Calf woman, a powerful tribal deity who figured prominently in the important ceremonies, not least the *wiwanyang wacipi* or 'Sun Dance'.

The origin of weaving the famed Chilkat blankets is explained in that tribe's story of Tsihooskwallaam (p. 58). Here, a beautiful and much admired woman chose to live in seclusion, high in the mountains, and became proficient in the art of weaving; in this tale, salmon, raven and martin take the role of tricksters, doing the opposite of their promises. Because of their actions, Tsihooskwallaam loses all her possessions but worse still, her hidden sanctuary is discovered and she dies of grief. After this tragedy, raven and martin – who were chief and son in disguise – distribute the blankets to the tribe in a great *Cutlas Potlach* (free gift) ceremony.

Likewise, a legacy from a mythical holy female, Spider Woman, is used to explain the origin of weaving among the Navajo. This sacred being is said to live in a hidden lair within the Canyon de Chelly in present-day Arizona. Spider webs were manifestations of her great ability at weaving,[3] and it was her spirit that guided the hands of the skilled Navajo women weavers. Powers of both sun and thunder are evoked in this mythical tale, which relates that Spider Woman first

PREVIOUS PAGE *Kwakiutl village scene showing houses, boats and totem poles, taken about 1895. These enormous carved totem poles, with their highly symbolic family and clan crests, were probably only fully developed towards the end of the eighteenth century when metal tools were introduced by Russian traders, although the symbolic statements made are far more ancient than this.*

A Hopi Kachina, date not recorded, but probably circa 1920. Kachinas represented the numerous spirit gods of the Hopi who figured prominently in and permeated through the whole of Hopi religion and ceremony. They were often used in the religious training of young children.

wove on a great loom that had been fabricated from lightning and the sun's rays (Woodhead, ed., p. 167).

While the gods are credited with the origin of such skills as weaving, in reality its development among the Navajo was due to contacts with the Pueblo people and later the Spanish and American traders. Thus, although origin myths do function as an explanation, the often fantasized narrative distinguishes it from any straightforward answer to an intellectual question: clearly, the educational value is embedded in the tribal lore and legend that it contained and that was perpetuated by the story teller. Thus, in the Nez Perce tale relating to the origin of fire (p. 65) it is pine that is credited with its creation in a bizarre story of trees and animals talking. However, as it unfolds, the fire – which we know is generated due to the friction between wood as in the ingenious and indispensable fire-drill – is explained. The importance of pine to the Subarctic people is also the subject of the Athapaskan myth (p. 55) relating to the origin of this wood from the phlegm of a man. With the Acoma explanation of the origin of summer and winter (p. 60) we have a lengthy and complicated tale relating to the spirits of winter, Shakok, and summer, Miochin, who finally strike a bargain that each would rule for half the year. Before this, however, through various bizarre escapades, they turn the northern animals wholly or partly white, and those in the south brown or black.

The atmosphere of the Northwest Coast with its grave houses, feasts in honor of the dead, rattles made from human skulls, and necklaces made from dead shamans' hands is vividly captured in the Tlingit myth (p. 50) relating to the origin of witchcraft and underlines much of the ceremony and ritual associated with this highly developed and complex cultural area.

ORIGIN OF WITCHCRAFT
(*Tlingit*)

I n the early days of Indian life there lived a young man who was a good hunter, and he had a very pretty young wife and a son, both of whom filled his heart with love. Their lives were happy as the flowers until one day the wife, while gathering wood in the forest, met the son of the chief, with whom she fell in love at the first glance. After this she met him every night by appointment on the seashore or in the woods. As days went on she feigned sickness, and calling her husband to her side, told him that she saw the spirits of her old friends coming to take her away, and that soon she would die and leave him, but made him promise not to burn her, but to put her body in a large box and place it in the gravehouse. That day she apparently died, when her last wish was carried out, and she was deposited in the small gravehouse in rear of the house. Night came on, and while the great feast (that it is customary with the Tlingit to give in honor of the dead) was being celebrated the chief's son went to the grave and assisted her to escape, and led her to his father's house, where she lived with him as his wife, but known only to his family. During the daytime she remained within doors, going out only under the shelter of darkness.

Many a winter evening the lonely hunter, sitting in his house with his little boy, would think about his dead wife, and all his heart would break out in tears. One day, returning from hunting and finding no fire, he sent his little boy into the chief's house to ask for some live coals to start his fire with. Upon entering the chief's house the little boy surprised his mother sitting by the fire. She saw him and immediately covered her face, but too late to prevent recognition. The boy went home and told his father that he had seen his mother, but his father told him to be quiet. He, however, insisted upon it, so that in the end the father's suspicions were aroused, and in the evening he stole softly to the chief's house, and looking through a chink discovered his wife sitting with her lover by the fire.

Upon returning home he sat down to think, how best to avenge this great wrong, and concluded to possess himself of a witch spirit: so the following night he took himself to the deadhouse and slept by a corpse, but the spirit did not come to him; he next killed a dog, and skinning it, slept one night in its skin, but again failed. Then he took a dead shaman's skull from the deadhouse and used it to drink out of, and the

The Tlingit chief, Shuky, lying in state at Fort Wrangle, Alaska; photograph taken in 1878. Shuky was a chief of the Southern Tlingit, who lived along the mainland and the sheltered waters of the Pacific coast. Death initiated eight days of mourning and for four days the deceased lay in state with lineage treasures piled beside him, as shown here.

Chief Shake's house, Tlingit village, at Fort Wrangle, Alaska. Photographed possibly by George Emmons, circa 1890. Tlingit country was rugged and the mainland from tidewater to high mountains was no more than 30 miles wide. The sea abounded in life: shellfish, sea mammals and fish. When sawed timber, nails, and carpentry tools became available from the 1890s onwards, many Tlingit built multi-family frame houses of the type shown here.

Da-yuc-bene, a Tlingit shaman curing a sick woman. Date not recorded but prior to 1906. The shaman was among the most important and powerful figures in his clan. He owed his powers to the spirits who were thought to enter his body and speak through him. Their major function was the detection of a witch (see myth), who was referred to as Nu-kw-sa-ti, 'master of sickness'.

next morning, going out, he suddenly fell down on the skull in a trance, and upon waking up the witch spirit had come to him, and he went home happy. Upon the coming of the night he returned to the shamans' graves, and there met many spirits of men and lovely maidens who danced and played with him, and every night afterwards he visited them and learned more and more of witchcraft.

After a while he took the bones of the dead shaman and made them into a necklace, which he put on. Then he killed a dog and made a blanket of its skin; then he took two shaman skulls, and filling them with pebbles, made rattles of them (all of these articles are used by the shamans in cases of witchcraft). He continued visiting the graves, associating with spirits and witches, and learned more and more daily, until he was able to fly, when he took the two skull rattles into his hands and flew to the chief's house. Upon reaching the smoke-hole he shook the rattles, and put every one in a sound sleep. Then he entered the house and saw his wife asleep in the arms of her lover. The next morning he went out and played: the people came out of their houses and all said, 'We slept very sound last night.' He afterwards went out into the woods and cut a small pole, which he sharpened at one end to a fine point; and the next night, when all were asleep, he flew down the smoke-hole of the chief's house and drove the sharpened stake through his faithless wife, killing her instantly, without noise. The next morning she was found dead, but no one knew who had killed her.

Now the hunter determined to give the witch spirit to his little boy, so that he could work any charm. He took the hand of an old dead shaman and hung it around the child's neck, and the little boy fell down in a trance, and the witch spirit came to him; then he went with his father every night to play with the spirits. The hunter now proposed to avenge himself on the chief's son. He instructed his little boy to watch his enemy and to secure his spittle, cut off a piece of his blanket, or wipe up his tracks; and with this and other material he made a small human figure, which he put inside a dead shaman, and as the image rotted, so sickness came to the chief's son, and as the image decayed, so the chief's son grew weaker and weaker until death came upon him. Then the hunter initiated his family into the mysteries of witchcraft, and it was thus that the witches originated.

ORIGIN OF THUNDER
(Passamaquoddy)

Once an Indian went forth to hunt. And he departed from the east branch of the Penobscot, and came to the head of another branch that leads into the east branch, and this he followed even to the foot of Mount Katahdin. And there he hunted many a day alone, and met no one, till one morning in midwinter he found a track of snow-shoes. So he returned to his camp; but the next day he met with it again in a far-distant place. And thus it was that, wherever he went, this track came to him every day. Then noting this, as a sign to be observed, he followed it, and went up the mountain, Katahdin, which means "the great mountain," until at last it was lost in a hard snow-shoe road made by many travelers. And since it was hard and even, he took off his agahmook, or snow-shoes, and went ever on and up the road; and it was a strange path and strange was its ending, for it stopped just before a high ledge, like an immense wall, on a platform

Wiwi-yokpa or Mary Elmanico, from the small Passamaquoddy tribe, which belonged to the Abenaki confederacy, an Algonquian linguistic group occupying the region around Passamaquoddy Bay and Schoodic Lake near the boundary between Maine and New Brunswick. Their mythology relates that the first man and woman were created out of stone but their chief god, Keshi Niwaskw was not satisfied and so he destroyed them creating two more out of wood. This equal standing of male and female was reflected in their social structure, thus, for example, in general council, both females and males decided the questions relating to war.

at its foot. And there were many signs there, as of many people, yet he saw no one. And as he stayed it seemed to grow stranger and stranger. At last he heard a sound as of footsteps coming, yet within the wall, when lo! a girl stepped directly out of the precipice upon the platform. But though she was beautiful beyond belief, he was afraid. And to his every thought she answered in words, and that so sweetly and kindly and cleverly that he was soon without fear, though he saw that she had powerful *m'téoulin*, or great magic power. And they being soon pleased one with the other, and wanting each other, she bade him accompany her, and that by walking directly though the rock. "Have no fear," said she, "but advance boldly!" So he obeyed, and lo! the rock was as the air, and it gave way as he went on. And ever as they went the maiden talked to him, answering his thoughts, so that he spoke not aloud.

And anon they came to a great cavern far within, and there was an old man seated by a fire, and the old man welcomed him. And he was very kindly treated by the strange pair all day; in all his life he had never been so happy. Now as the night drew near, the old man said to his daughter, "Can you hear aught of your brothers?" Then she went out to the terrace, and, returning, said, "No." Then anon he asked her again, and she, going and returning as before, replied, "Now I hear them coming." Then they listened, when lo! there came, as at the door without, a crash of thunder with a flash of lightning, and out of the light stepped two young men of great beauty, but like giants, stupendous and of awful mien. And, like their father, their eyebrows were of stone, while their cheeks were as rocks.

And the hunter was told by their sister that when they went forth, which was every few days, their father said to them, "Sons, arise! it is time now for you to go forth over the world and save our friends. Go not too far near the trees, but if you see aught that is harmful to those whom we love, strike, and spare not!" Then when they went forth they flew on high, among the clouds; and thus it is that the Thunder and Lightning, whose home is in the mighty Katahdin, are made. And when the thunder strikes, the brothers are shooting at the enemies of their friends.

Now when the day was done the hunter returned to his home, and when there, found he had been gone seven years.

A typical Passamaquoddy birch bark lodge photographed in the Zoological Park, Washington, in 1896. This was constructed by two Passamaquoddy Indians, Joseph Thomas and Newell Thomas, at the instigation of the Bureau of American Ethnology to illustrate aboriginal architecture and domestic life. The materials were of birch bark and willow poles tied together with ash splints and spruce roots. All the cutting and shaping was done with stone tools and fire.

Lower Ahtna babies, photograph taken about 1903. They are in a baby carrier, probably made of birch bark, which has been stitched with spruce root. It is then padded and an absorbent material, such as moss or grass, is added (this can be seen at the left). The infant's legs then hang over the front, held in place by a vertical tongue. Note the attractive floral beaded carrying strap (right).

ORIGIN OF THE PINE
(Athapaskan)

There were a number of Indians in a camp who went away one by one and were lost. At last only one remained, and he also decided to leave the camp. He soon encountered a wolverine, which said, "I know who you are; you will have to go before me." As they went along they came out upon the river at a point where the bank was very steep. The wolverine said, "You must slide down." So the Indian slid down the bank, and the wolverine ran around through a ravine. When the man reached the bottom, he caused his nose to bleed, and put some of the blood on a spear, and then laid down and feigned death. When the wolverine reached the spot where the man lay, he took him up and carried him to his camp across the river. After placing him in the middle of the camp he began to sharpen his knife. The man soon opened his eyes and looked for a stick; when he found a stick he sprang up and killed all the wolverines except one young one which ran up a tree. The man blew his nose and threw the phlegm at the tree, and was transformed into a pine. The wolverine then said, "That will do for your arrows; now you must leave me alone."

Group of Ahtna, probably in a temporary hunting camp, photographed about 1903. In the nineteenth century, Ahtna territory included some 23,000 square miles of the Copper River valley in Southern Alaska. A variety of habitations were used, depending on the duration of stay. A skin or canvas covered domed structure, of the type shown here, was used in the winter camps. Spruce branches served as tent flooring.

THE CHILKAT BLANKET
(*Chilkat*)

Many generations ago there lived a very beautiful woman, named Tsihooskwallaam, who had chosen to live far away from her tribespeople in the mountain wilderness of the great Chilkat country.

Tsihooskwallaam had many admirers among her own tribespeople, who would have married her, but Tsihooskwallaam preferred to live a secluded life from her own tribespeople.

She selected as a place to live an unknown lake far away from the haunts of men, believing that her people would never find her, and there she settled down to study the art and craft of weaving blankets. The outlet of the lake was a stream in which there were many rapids and falls, and which was frequented by salmon, which made their way to the lake.

The salmon sought many times to find Tsihooskwallaam, and when they found her she asked them as a special favor to help her by not telling anyone of her new *illahee* (home). When the salmon returned to the salt chuck (water), they told of Tsihooskwallam's new home and the great chief and his son set out with all possible speed, after preparing their war canoe and providing themselves with *muck-a-muck* (eatables) and many *skookum* (strong) river men, to find her. Traveling according to the direction the salmon had given them, they arrived at the lake, and the chief, whose name was Num-Kil-slas, proposed to Tsihooskwallaam that she marry his son Gunnuckets, to which she consented, providing the chief and his son would agree to remain with her and never leave the premises during her life; to which they agreed. After the marriage and feast, they settled down to work on blankets. They asked Tsihooskwallaam where she obtained the material for making these blankets, and she answered that she hunted mountain goats in the mountains, from which

OPPOSITE Sitka Jake, *a Tlingit (Sitka) Indian in a chilkat dance blanket and headdress, probably photographed circa 1900. He was known as a generous potlach giver, one of the great winter ceremonies of the Northwest Coast tribes. The word was derived from the Nootka,* patshatl, *'giving' or 'gift', and part of the ceremony involved the giving away of vast quantities of goods, generally blankets such as the magnificent one shown here.*

BELOW Haida *potlach dancers at Klinkwan, Alaska, photograph taken about 1900. Note the superb blankets worn by three of the men. These were actually made by Tlingit women (a tribe closely related to the Haida) who lived in the village of Chilkat at the mouth of the Copper River, Alaska. Hence the term 'chilkat' blanket – a much coveted trade item and a sign of considerable wealth.*

she derived the material; the next day at *tenas sun* (day break) she would take Gunnuckets with her, where he could hunt the mountain sheep for her. Now Tsihooskwallaam's house was very large, being built of big timber forty to sixty feet in length and finely decorated inside with many beautiful woods, such as were unknown to the people of her tribe. Gunnuckets and his father were very envious, and being bad at heart, began to plan how to steal all the woman's blankets and belongings. Gunnuckets told his father to take stock of what there was in the premises, and arrange it all in bundles so that between them they could take it during his wife's absence. The next day while Tsihooskwallaam and her husband had gone hunting sheep in the mountains, Num-Kil-slas took stock of all there was on the premises, and arranged everything in bundles so that he and his son could carry everything away when the opportunity offered. Meanwhile Gunnuckets made an excuse to his wife for returning to the house alone, and upon his arrival at the house both he and his father turned to their original characters. Num-Kil-slas became a raven and Gunnuckets a martin. The raven took many bundles of valuable blankets in his beak, while the martin took all he possibly could carry in his jaws, and they started with great speed to carry away all they could. At night Tsihooskwallaam returned to the house and found she had been deceived by her husband and his father, and how they had stolen all her valuables, but the loss of the valuables did not worry her as much as the knowledge of being exposed to her tribespeople. She wandered away into the woods thinking that she might possibly overtake them and regain her possessions and valuables, but she failed in her efforts and died from grief.

Num-Kil-slal and Gunnuckets reached their destination with all the blankets and valuables and distributed them as a *Cutlas Potlach* (free gift) to all the people of the Chilkat tribe, after which the people learned to make these wonderful blankets which are used up to the present time, only by chiefs in their dances and during the tribal ceremonies of the Chilkat Indians.

ORIGIN OF SUMMER AND WINTER
(Acoma)

The oldest tradition of the people of Acoma and Laguna indicates that they lived on some island; that their homes were destroyed by tidal waves, earthquakes, and red-hot stones from the sky. They fled and landed on a low, swampy coast. From here they migrated to the northwest, and wherever they made a long stay they built a "White City" (Kush-kut-ret).

The fifth White City was built somewhere in southern Colorado or northern New Mexico. The people were obliged to leave it on account of cold, drought, and famine.

The first governor of Acoma had a daughter named Co-chin-ne-na-ko: she was the wife of Shakok, the spirit of Winter. After he came to live with them the seasons grew colder and colder; the snow and ice stayed longer, the corn would no longer mature, and the people were compelled to live on cactus leaves (e-mash-chu) and other wild plants.

One day Co-chin-ne-na-ko went out to gather cactus leaves and burn off the thorns so that she could take them home for food. She had a leaf singed and was eating it, when upon looking up she saw a young man coming towards her. He had on a yellow shirt, woven of corn silk, a belt, and a tall pointed hat; green leggings made of the green moss which grows in the springs and ponds, and moccasins beautifully embroidered with flowers and butterflies. In his hand he carried an ear of green corn. He came up and saluted her. She replied. Then he asked her what she was eating. She told him that the people were almost starved; that no corn would grow; and that they were all compelled to live on cactus leaves.

"Here," he said, "take this ear of corn and eat it, and I will go and bring you an armful to take home with you." He started and was soon out of sight, going towards the south. In a very short time, however, he returned, bringing a large bundle of green corn (ken-utch), which he laid at her feet. Co-chin-ne-na-ko asked him where he had found the corn, and if it grew near by. He replied that he had brought it from his home,

The Rainbow Spring referred to by the Zuni as
K'iapkwainakwin, 'place whence flow the hot
waters'. This spring was considered sacred to the Zuni
Shalako gods who figured prominently in rainmaking
ceremonies (see image on p. 63). This is at Ojo
Caliente (Spanish: 'warm spring'), which is a Zuni
summer village about fourteen miles southwest of Zuni
pueblo, New Mexico.

A Zuni altar showing the cloud symbols and fetishes of the Rain Priest. Photograph taken prior to 1898 at the Pueblo of Zuni in New Mexico. Temporary altars of this type were a characteristic of the Pueblos; a direction or cloud altar often consisted of a bowl surrounded with ears of corn pointing towards the cardinal points.

far to the south, where the corn grows and the flowers bloom all the year. "Oh, how I would like to see your country; will you not take me with you to your home?" she said. "Your husband, Shakok, the Spirit of Winter, would be angry if I should take you away," he said. She said, "I do not love him, he is cold; ever since he came here no corn will grow, no flowers will bloom, and the people are compelled to live on prickly-pear leaves."

"Well," said he, "take the bundle of corn home with you and do not throw any of the husks outside of the door; then come tomorrow and I will bring you more. I will meet you here." Then, bidding her farewell, he left again for his home in the south. Co-chin-ne-na-ko took the bundle of corn he had given her and started to go home to the town. She had not gone far when she met her sisters, for becoming alarmed at her long stay they had come out to look for her. They were very much surprised on seeing her with an armful of green corn instead of cactus leaves. Co-chin-ne-na-ko told them how the young man had come to her and brought the corn. So they helped her carry it home. When they arrived their father and mother were wonderfully surprised, but pleased to see them bringing big ears of green corn instead of cactus leaves. They asked Co-chin-ne-na-ko where she had found it, and she told them, as she had already told her sisters, that a young man, whom she minutely described, had brought her the corn, and had asked her to meet him at the same place on the following day, and that he would accompany her home. "It is Miochin," said her father, "it is Miochin." "It is surely Miochin," said her mother. "Bring him home with you by all means." The next day Co-chin-ne-na-ko went to the place where she had met Miochin, for he really was Miochin, the Spirit of Summer. He was already there waiting for her. He had big bundles of corn.

Between them they carried it to the town, and there was enough to feed all the people of Acoma, and Miochin was welcomed at the house of the governor. In the evening, as was his custom, Shakok, the Spirit of

Winter, and husband of Co-chin-ne-na-ko, returned from the north where he spend the days playing with the north wind, and with the snow and sleet and hail. He came in a blinding storm of snow, sleet, and hail.

On reaching the town he knew that Miochin was there, and called out to him, "Ha, Miochin, are you here?" Miochin advanced to meet him. "Ha, Miochin, now I will destroy you." "Ha, Shakok, I will destroy you," answered Miochin. Shakok stopped, and as Miochin advanced towards him the snow and hail melted and the fierce wind turned to a summer breeze. Shakok was covered with frost, icicles hung all about him, but as Miochin advanced towards him the frost melted, the icicles dropped off, and his clothing was revealed. It was made of dry bleached rushes (ska-ra-ska-ru-ka). Shakock said, "I will not fight you now, but will meet you here in four days from now and fight you till one or the other is beaten. The winner shall have Co-chin-ne-na-ko." With that Shakok left in a rage.

The wind again roared and shook the very walls, but the people were warm in their houses. Miochin was there. Next day he left for his home in the south. Arriving there he made preparations for the meeting with Shakok. He first sent an eagle to his friend Yat-chum-me Moot, who lived in the west, asking him to come and help him in his fight with Shakok. Then he called all the birds, insects, and four-legged animals that live in summer lands. All these he called to help him. The bat (Pick-le-ke) was his advance guard and his shield, as the tough skin of the bat could best withstand the sleet and hail that Shakok would throw at him. On the third day Yat-chum-me kindled his fires, and heated the thin flat stones that he was named after. Then big black clouds of smoke rolled up from the south and covered the sky. When Shakok left he went to the north and called to him all the winter birds and the four-legged animals of the winter lands. He called these all to come and help him in the coming battle. The magpie (Shro-ak-ah) was his shield and advance guard. On the morning of the fourth day the two enemies could be seen coming. In the north the black storm clouds of winter, with snow, sleet and hail were bringing Shakok to the battle. In the south, Yat-chum-me piled more wood on his fires and great puffs of steam and smoke arose and formed into clouds. These were coming fast towards Acoma, and the place where the fight was to take place, and were bringing Miochin, the Spirit of Summer. The thick smoke of Yat-chum-me's fires blackened all the animals Miochin had with him, and that is why the animals in the south are black or brown. Forked blazes of lightning shot out of the clouds that were bringing Miochin. Each came fast. Shakok from the north; Miochin from the south. At last they reached the town, and the flashes from the clouds singed the feathers and hair on the birds and animals that came with Shakok, turning them white; that is the reason why all the animals and birds that live in the north

The Shalako dancers who were considered the Giant Courier Gods of the Rainmakers and messengers of the Rainmaker Priests. This photograph taken in the late 1890s, shows part of the Shalako House Blessing Ceremony, the dancers crossing a field to the ceremonial grounds at the Zuni Pueblo in New Mexico.

are white, or have some white about them. Shakok and Miochin were now close together. From the north Shakok threw snow-flakes, sleet, and hail that hissed through the air a blinding storm. In the south the big black clouds rolled along, and from Yat-chum-me's fires still rose up great puffs of smoke and steam that heated the air and melted Shakok's snow and sleet and hail, and compelled him to fall back. At last Shakok called for a truce. Miochin agreed, and the winds stopped and the snow and rain ceased falling.

They met at the wall of Acoma, and Shakok said, "I am defeated; you are the winner; Co-chin-ne-na-ko is yours." Then they agreed that Shakok should rule during half of the year, and Miochin during the other half, and that neither should trouble the other thereafter.

Ever since then one half of the year has been cold and the other half warm.

ABOVE *Joseph Ratunda, a Nez Perce boy, photographed probably at Lapwai, Idaho, about 1900. The religious beliefs of the Nez Perce prior to the introduction of Christianity put great emphasis on animal powers, and were based on acute observation of animal characteristics. This fine little boy's costume is embellished with horse and porcupine hair roach, and an otter-skin breast band, from which hang skins of the weasel, an animal recognized for its speed and survival powers.*

LEFT *Tomason (Timothy), Nez Perce headman, photographed in Washington in 1868 and wearing a magnificent traditional costume, heavily quilled and beaded. When the missionaries first arrived among the Nez Perce in the 1840s, they found several of the leaders were willing to listen to the teachings of Christianity. Tomason became one of the first converts and changed his name to Timothy. Other leaders, such as Joseph, however, became disillusioned, and this led to a split in the Nez Perce tribe, ultimately one group making a heroic, but abortive, retreat to Canada in 1877.*

RIGHT *Beadwork on a woman's bag, probably Nez Perce, and dating from circa 1890. The figure is obviously a butterfly, the central triangular motif undoubtedly representing a cocoon. Metamorphosis was a widely recognized phenomenon throughout North America, having symbolic associations relating to renewal and regeneration.*

BELOW *A cornhusk bag, Nez Perce, probably circa 1890. These finely woven bags were popular trade items. They were mainly used to store camas roots and wild turnips; however, they even turn up in Blackfeet medicine bundles and were much favored by the Crow for storing clothing and beaded items. While mainly twisted cornhusk, some of the pattern is made up from coloured wool.*

ORIGIN OF FIRE: HOW BEAVER STOLE FIRE
(*Nez Perce*)

Long ago there were no people in the world. Animals and trees talked just as men do now. They also walked about. Now in those days, Pine Trees had the secret of fire. They would tell no one else. No one could have a fire, no matter how cold it was, unless he were a Pine. One winter it was so cold that the animals almost froze to death. Then they called a council. They wanted to steal fire from the Pine Trees.

Now on Grande Ronde River, the Pine Trees were also holding a great council. They had built a large fire to warm themselves. Guards were put around the fire to keep off all animals. But Beaver hid under the bank, near the fire, before the guards took their places, so they did not see him. After a while a live coal rolled down the bank near Beaver. He hid it in his breast and ran away. The Pine Trees started after him. When they caught up near him, Beaver dodged from side to side. Other times he ran straight ahead. That is why Grande Ronde River winds from side to side in some places. In other places it is straight.

When they had run a long way, the Pine Trees grew tired. They stopped on the river banks. So many stopped there, and so close together, that even today hunters can hardly get through the trees. A few kept on after Beaver and stopped here and there. These also remain here and there on the river bank.

A few Pine Trees kept close after Beaver. So did Cedar. Cedar said, "I will run to the top of that hill. I will see how far ahead he is." So Cedar ran to the top of the hill. Beaver was far ahead. He was just diving into Big Snake River where Grande Ronde joins it. Beaver swam across Big Snake River and gave fire to the Willows on the opposite bank. Farther on he gave fire to the Birches and to other trees. So these woods have fire in them. Ever since then animals and Indians can get fire from these woods by rubbing two pieces together.

Cedar still stands all alone on the very top of the hill. He is very old. His top is dead. The chase was a long one. You can see that because there are no other cedars within a hundred miles of him. Old men of the tribes point him out to the children. They say, "There is Old Cedar. He stands just where he stopped when he chased Beaver."

Gahano or 'Hanging Flower' better known as Caroline Parker, a Seneca woman photographed about 1870. She was the daughter of the mixed-blood Seneca, General Eli Samuel Parker, Hasanoanda 'Coming to the Front', who was a close associate of General Grant. Note the plant design on the skirt worn by Gahano, possibly a symbolic reference to the Seneca De-o-ha-ko.

ORIGIN OF CORN
(*Iroquois*)

A fine young man lived on a small hill, and being there alone he wished to marry. He had flowing robes, and wore long and nodding plumes, so that he was very beautiful to behold. Every morning and evening he came out of his quiet house, and three times he sang, "*Che hen, Che hen. Sone ke kwah no wah ho ten ah you ke neah. Say it, Say it. Some one I will marry*;" and he thought he cared not at all who it might be. For a long time he kept this up, every morning and night, and still he was a lonesome young man.

At last a tall young woman came, with long hair neatly braided behind, as is the Indian style. Her beads shone like drops of dew, and her flowing green mantle was adorned with large golden bells. The young man ceased to sing, and she said, "I am the one for whom you have been looking so long, and I am

The front of a house of the Gens Gi'gilkum people of the region of Alert Bay, British Columbia. Photograph possibly by C. O. Hastings prior to 1889. The characteristic Kwakiutl painting depicts the Thunderbird-lifting-a-whale design, and merges realistic and geometric styles. Such crests, together with their ritual privileges and accompanying myths, were transferred through successive marriages.

come to marry you." But he looked at her and said, "No! you are not the one. You wander so much from home, and run over the ground so fast, that I cannot keep by your side. I cannot have you." So the pumpkin maiden went away, and the young man was still alone, but kept on singing morning and night, hoping his bride would come.

One day there appeared a slender young woman, of graceful form and fair of face. Her beautiful mantle was spotted here and there with lovely clusters of flowers, and groups of bangles hung upon it. She heard the song and drew near the singer. Then she said she could love dearly one so manly and would marry him if he would love her in turn. The song ceased; he looked at her and was pleased, and said she was just the one he had wished, and for whom he had waited so long. They met with a loving embrace, and ever since the slender bean twines closely around the corn, he supporting her and she cherishing him. Perhaps it might be added that they are not divided in death, for beans make a part of Indian corn bread.

THE FIRST TOTEM POLE
(*Kwakiutl*)

Once there was a chief who had never had a dance. All the other chiefs had big dances, but Wakiash none. Therefore Wakiash was unhappy. He thought for a long while about the dance. Then he went up into the mountains to fast. Four days he fasted. On the fourth day he fell asleep. Then something fell on his breast. It was a green frog. Frog said, "Wake up." Then Wakiash woke up. He looked about to see where he was. Frog said, "You are on Raven's back. Raven will fly around the world with you."

A Koskimo woman photographed prior to 1895. The Koskimo were an important Kwakiutl tribe who inhabited the shores of the Quatsino Sound on Vancouver Island. Note the high-domed skull of this woman; it was a tradition among the Kwakiutl that female infants of high-ranking families had their heads reshaped by applying pressure to the head when they were in the cradle. This 'sugar loaf' shape is typical in the region

Carved totem, Northwest Coast, possibly Kwakiutl, late nineteenth century. The upper figure is a stylized raven, a bird recognised for its cleverness and cunning; at the middle is a salmon and below a bear symbol. Thus, sky, earth, and underwater powers are referred to here.

So Raven flew. Raven flew all around the world. Raven showed Wakiash everything in the world. On the fourth day, Raven flew past a house with a totem pole in front of it. Wakiash could hear singing in the house. Wakiash wished he could take the totem pole and the house with him. Now Frog knew what Wakiash was thinking. Frog told Raven. Raven stopped and Frog told Wakiash to hide behind the door. Frog said, "When they dance, jump out into the room."

The people in the house began to dance. They were animal people. But they could not sing or dance. One said, "Something is the matter. Some one is near us."

Chief said, "Let one who can run faster than the flames go around the house and see."

So Mouse went. Mouse could go anywhere, even into a box. Now Mouse looked like a woman, she had taken off her animal clothes. Mouse ran out, but Wakiash caught her.

Wakiash said, "Wait, I will give you something." So he gave her a piece of Mountain goat's fat. Wakiash said to Mouse, "I want the totem pole and the house. I want the dances and the songs."

Mouse said, "Wait until I come again."

Mouse went back into the house. She said, "I could find nobody." So the animal people tried again to dance. They tried three times. Each time, Chief sent Mouse out to see if some one was near. Each time, Mouse talked with Wakiash. The third time Mouse said, "When they begin to dance, jump into the room."

So the animal people began to dance. Then Wakiash sprang into the room. The dancers were ashamed. They had taken off their animal clothes and looked like men. So the animal people were silent. Then Mouse said, "What does this man want?" Now Wakiash wanted the totem pole and the house. He wanted the dances and the songs. Mouse knew what Wakiash was thinking. Mouse told the animal people.

Chief said, "Let the man sit down. We will show him how to dance." So they danced. Then Chief asked Wakiash what kind of a dance he would like to choose. They were using masks for the dance. Wakiash wanted the Echo mask and the Little Man mask-the little man who talks, talks, and quarrels with others. Mouse told the people what Wakiash was thinking.

Then Chief said, "You can take the totem pole and the house also. You can take the masks and dances, for one dance." Then Chief folded up the house very small. He put it in a dancer's headdress. Chief said, "When you reach home, throw down this bundle. The house will unfold and you can give a dance."

Then Wakiash went back to Raven. Wakiash climbed on Raven's back and went to sleep. When he awoke, Raven and Frog were gone. Wakiash was alone. It was night and the tribe was asleep. Then Wakiash threw down the bundle. Behold! the house and totem pole were there. The whale painted on the house was blowing. The animals on the totem pole were making noises. At once the tribe woke up. They came to see Wakiash. Wakiash found he had been gone four years instead of four days.

Then Wakiash gave a great dance. He taught the people the songs. Echo came to the dance. He repeated all the sounds they made. When they finished the dance, behold! the house was gone. It went back to the animal people. Thus all the chiefs were ashamed because Wakiash had the best dance.

Then Wakiash made out of wood a house and another totem pole. They called it Kulakuyuwish, "the pole that holds up the sky."

Jack Red Cloud, son of Makhpia-sha or 'Red Cloud', a principal chief of the Oglala Lakota in South Dakota. Wearing a fine eagle feather headdress and beaded shirt, he carries a typical Sioux pipe with a long stem decorated with porcupine quillwork. The head is made of catlinite, a red stone that Sioux mythology relates was a gift from the Great Spirit. Note the Ulysses S. Grant peace medal (1871) worn by Red Cloud.

THE ORIGIN OF PIPESTONE
(*Sioux*)

At an ancient time the Great Spirit, in the form of a large bird, stood upon the wall of rock and called all the tribes around him, and breaking out a piece of the red stone formed it into a pipe and smoked it, the smoke rolling over the whole multitude. He then told his red children that this red stone was their flesh, that they were made from it, that they must all smoke to him through it, that they must use it for nothing but pipes: and as it belonged alike to all the tribes, the ground was sacred, and no weapons must be used or brought upon it.

ORIGIN OF THE WAMPUM
(*Seneca*)

Many, many moons ago, when our old men were but whispers in the woods and their fathers and mothers played the game of sticks at the lake side and the fish swam to meet the spear, a great trouble came upon the Senecas. From the north came a warlike tribe, the Chippewa, and fell upon the villages and killed young warriors and took away the most beautiful maidens. Many war parties followed brave chiefs to find and rescue the maidens, but alas! they, too, were swept away. The head chief, the wise Da-ga-now-e-da, called a council, and taking his stand before his old men and warriors, spoke long and earnestly of the ruin wrought by the fierce Chippewa and the futility of giving battle to so strong a people. Thus he recommended: "Send my son, the eloquent and brave Ha-o-a-tha, southward to the tribes friendly to us and lay before them this vital matter, and that by union we may be able to break the power of these fierce northern warriors and peace will ensue to our people." The old man smoked in silence until a venerable chief arose and in a wise speech gave his approval to the words of his chief. Murmurs of satisfaction came from all quarters and the council adjourned. In the gray of the dawn young Ha-o-a-tha stepped into his light canoe and turning his face toward the south, departed upon his journey. When the noon day sun beat upon him he turned the bow of his canoe to the margin of the stream and, as the light craft shelved the beach, he stepped ashore, and, after a frugal meal, sat long and silently, thinking over his mission, and, fully realizing the great importance of presenting the case in the most appealing form, rehearsed in his mind what words and arguments he should use. His thoughts flowed slowly, but at last he felt satisfied and stepping aboard his canoe he shot out into the stream. As the current caught and carried him along he sought to grasp again the ideas that had so recently presented themselves. Alas! they were gone, and try as he would they did not return. Again he turned to the shore and as the canoe grated the pebbles he plunged his paddle into the sandy beach and brought it dripping across the boat. Bowing his head in his hands he was again lost in meditation. Slowly the ideas came, but would not remain. Sadly he turned his head, and his gaze fixed upon the blade of the paddle, on which were some small shells glittering in the sunlight. Picking up a small white shell he idly turned it in his palm; a small hole through its centre attracted his gaze, and fingering the fringe of his girdle, he slowly strung the shell upon the thong. As quick as a flash came an inspiration. A thought was represented by the small white shell. Another black shell was drawn into place beside the former one. At last his speech was a fixture in his mind, and as he ran the shells through his fingers his thoughts ran in unison. Gaily he left the shore, and before night-fall was among the sought for allies of his father's tribe. The council met, and never before had the chiefs listened to such eloquence. The day was won. Departing home, young Ha-o-a-tha carried the assurance of assistance to his people, and soon runners arrived from the on-coming allies, who recited the wonderful and eloquent appeal of the young chief. To his father he confided his secret and thus was adopted the conveyance of messages and thought by means of pierced shells or wampum.

ABOVE *A group of Iroquois chiefs explaining their wampum belts. This photograph was taken about 1871 on their reserve near Brantford in Canada and shows chiefs of the Onondaga, Mohawk and Seneca. At the extreme right is Seneca Johnson, Kanonkeredawih, a Seneca chief. Note his turban-like headdress, probably a finger-woven sash, wrapped around his head. Wampum belts were made to commemorate particular events and acted as memory aids, the keeper being charged with the responsibility of remembering particular parts of the story.*

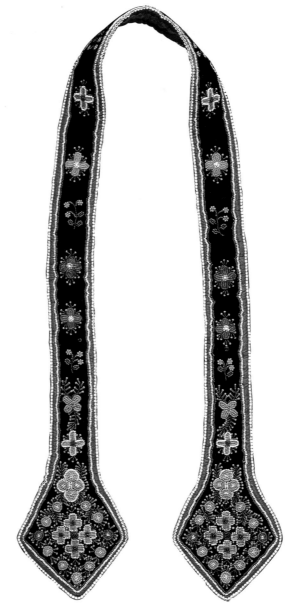

An Iroquois sash, sign of status and rank. This probably dates from the mid-nineteenth century. Black velvet, on which the beaded motifs are worked, early replaced the traditional black buckskin. Red silk and white pony beads border both the band and decorative triangular flaps that make up the sash.

A magnificent Iroquois Glengarry hat dating from circa 1870. These were a direct copy from Scottish highlander hats although the beadworked motifs are typical Iroquois for this period. Note the two shades of one colour in the designs, so characteristic of this style of Iroquois beadwork. The hat is surmounted by a large plume from the tail of a golden eagle.

73

— 3 —

Sky Powers

THE NORTH AMERICAN INDIANS have a large share of animistic beliefs and attribute supernatural powers to a variety of things. Thus, mountains, rivers, stones, bluffs, and the like have spirits, either in a personified form or as the seat of great powers. Out of this welter of supernatural forces, skypowers are prominent and many myths throughout the continent refer to powers received from the stars (p. 87), sun, and moon (p. 81), and while references to the Pleiades (pp. 85, 90) are also widespread, not surprisingly such phenomena as the Northern Lights (p. 83) and the Celestial Bear (p. 78) are more characteristic of the Arctic and Subarctic regions.

Although the Huron and Iroquois of the Northeastern Woodlands referred to the north star as 'the star that always stands still' in general they tended to ignore star phenomenain favor of the sun and moon, which held a prominent place in both their customs and mythology – medallions of wampum beads, for example, which were sometimes given to signify honest and open interaction in diplomatic transactions, displayed a circular image of the sun with rays emanating from the surface.

Permeating through the Huron spiritual universe, was the supernatural force that they referred to as Oki. It was Oki, as the dominant sky spirit, who held sway over the weather and gave force to the winds and waves. Seldom did the Huron and other Iroquoian speaking people fail to invoke this power in their treaty-making, ceremonies, and other solemn occasions; to ignore such powers courted sickness, hunger, or death, as is the fate of those who dared challenge the sky powers in the Salishan myth (p. 88).

Undoubtedly, the two star groups that play the most conspicuous roles in Algonquian legends – be they the Chippewa of the northern Woodlands, the Cree of the Subarctic, or the Cheyenne and Blackfeet of the Great Plains – were the Pleiades and Great Bear. Two such myths on the Pleiades (pp. 85, 90) and one on the Bear (p. 78) are reproduced here. Hardin (p. 37) points to the fact that early missionaries were greatly impressed by the Algonquian's reference to the Great Bear, the deluge, a passage through divided water, a hero miraculously born, and types of baptism, confession and communion, as well as the use of the Cross as a sacred symbol. This parallel mythology with the Old World led them to suggest that an apostle had at some time visited the continent (see also introduction to Chapter 1).

While the same story might be found in different cultural areas, each version frequently displayed an entirely different emphasis. Obviously, the setting was distinct but additionally the main points of the tale were elaborated by the different tribes, so taking on a local coloring that could only be understood in relation to the whole culture and that often served to explain ritual and ceremony. Thus, the myth of the star husband occurs on the Plains, in the Northeast and in British Columbia. The Plains tribes tell of two maidens who go to dig roots and camp out; they see two stars and wish to be married to them. The next morning they find themselves in the sky and married to the stars but now they are forbidden to dig large roots. However, they ignore the directive, dig a root out of the sky and climb through the hole to earth. There are variants on the subsequent events; one version emphasizes the adventures of the women after they return, another the feats of the child conceived by one of them. This leads to a series of myths, which in the case of the Blackfeet refer to the Sun Dance and the cultural hero, Scar Face. The central events are completely changed in the story told by the tribes in British Columbia. Here, the girls of a village build a house in which they play and one day discuss the stars thinking how happy they must be because they are able to view the whole world. When they awake the next morning, they are in the sky before the beautifully carved and painted house of an exalted chief; several men now appear feigning friendship but they kill most of the girls by sucking out their brains and only two daughters of the chief survive, the elder of whom subsequently marries the chief of the stars. Finally, she is sent back to earth laden with regalia and accoutrements for a ceremony that becomes the property of the woman's family – a recurring theme in this region, which emphasizes the acquisition of ritual from the sky powers.

Star motifs are commonly found in the art of the Plains tribes and among the most frequently mentioned in their mythology, was Venus, referred to as the 'Morning Star'.

The Skidi band of the Pawnee used a symbol of the Morning Star in the decoration of a baby's cradle, the explanation for which is given in the myth of 'How Evening Star's Daughter was Overcome'. In this myth, the gods built an earth lodge and Evening Star sent her daughter to rule the lodge. Evening Star was the spouse of Morning Star and wanted women to be higher than men.[4] In a village in the east, a poor boy was commissioned by a strangely dressed man to go and marry the girl; he was to have a moccasin with the symbol of Morning Star on it to serve as his helper. As he went on his journey, many obstacles presented themselves to the boy.

PREVIOUS PAGE *Ahtna children and (probably) grandmother, photograph taken about 1903. Note the use of bone buttons for decoration, a popular item at this time. The environment of the Ahtna was rugged due to glacial action, the climate varied dramatically: minus 30°F or lower during winter and 90°F or more in summer.*

Fortunately, each time he threw his moccasin the obstacle was obliterated. The girl herself put an obstacle in his way, and the boy had to return to her with a baby cradle. At this point, Morning Star appeared, and he himself got the cradle. After receiving it, the girl made other demands to keep the boy from sleeping with her, but at every turn Morning Star solved the problem. One final obstacle presented itself. The girl's vagina was filled with rattlesnake teeth. Morning Star warned the boy that he must smash the teeth with a rock before he lay down with her. This the boy did and thereupon the girl became a human being. As a reward for all this help, Morning Star asked for human sacrifice. One young maiden captured from an enemy camp was to be sacrificed annually by the Pawnee to Morning Star.[5] A further request made by Morning Star was that his symbol be placed on the top of each baby board in addition to being used in other places (Dorsey).

The Morning Star motif on a Crow headstall, circa 1880. Such star motifs, or those in the form of a Maltese Cross, were particularly popular with the Crow, Cheyenne, and Arapaho. They were considered to be symbols of protective power.

THE CELESTIAL BEAR
(*Algonquian*)

Late in spring, the bear waking from her long winter sleep, leaves her rocky hillside den and descends to the ground in search of food. Instantly the sharp-eyed chickadee perceives her, and, being too small to undertake the pursuit alone, calls the other hunters to his aid. Together the seven start after the bear, the chickadee with his pot being placed between two of the larger birds so that he may not lose his way. All the hunters are hungry for meat after the short rations of winter and so they pursue eagerly, but throughout the summer the bear flees across the northern horizon and the pursuit continues. In the autumn, one by one, the hunters in the rear begin to lose their trail. First of all the two owls, heavier and clumsier of wing than the other birds, disappear from the chase. But you must not laugh when you hear how Kopkéch, the smaller owl, failed to secure a share of the bear meat, and you must not imitate his rasping cry, for if you disregard either warning, be sure that wherever you are, as soon as you are asleep he will descend from the sky with a birch bark torch and set fire to whatever clothing covers you. Next the blue jay and the pigeon also lose the trail and drop out of the chase. This leaves only the robin, the chickadee, and the moose bird, but they continue the pursuit, and at last, about mid-autumn, they overtake their prey.

Brought to bay, the bear rears up on her hind feet and prepares to defend herself, but the robin pierces her with an arrow and she falls over upon her back. The robin being himself very thin at this season is intensely eager to eat some of the bear's fat as soon as possible. In his haste he leaps upon his victim, and becomes covered with blood. Flying to a maple-tree near at hand in the land of the sky, he tries to shake off this blood. He succeeds in getting it all off save a spot upon his breast. "That spot," says the garrulous chickadee, "you will carry as long as your name is robin."

But the blood which he does shake off spatters far and wide over the forests of earth below, and hence we see each autumn the blood-red tints on the foliage; it is reddest on the maples, because trees on earth follow the appearance of the trees in the sky, and the sky maple received most of the blood. The sky is just the same as the earth, only up above, and older.

Some time after these things happened to the robin, the chickadee arrived on the scene. These two birds cut up the bear, built a fire, and placed some of the meat over it to cook. Just as they were about to begin to eat, the moose bird put in his appearance.

He had almost lost the trail, but when he regained it he had not hurried, because he knew that it would take his companions some time to cook the meat after the bear was slain, and he did not mind missing that part of the affair so long as he arrived in time for a full share of the food. Indeed, he was so impressed with the advantages of this policy, that ever since then he has ceased to hunt for himself, preferring to follow after hunters and share their spoils. And so, whenever a bear or a moose or other animal is killed today in the woods of Megumaage, Micmac Land, you will see him appear to demand his share. That is why the other birds named him Mikchagogwech, He-who-comes-in-at-the-last-moment, and the Micmacs say there are some men who ought to be called that too.

However that may be, the robin and chickadee, being generous, willingly shared their food with the moose bird. Before they ate, the robin and moose bird danced around the fire, while the chickadee stirred the pot. Such was the custom in the good old times, when Micmacs were brothers all to all and felt it a duty to share their food together, and to thank each other and the Universal Spirit for their present happiness.

But this does not end the story of the bear, though one might think so. Through the winter her skeleton lies upon its back in the sky, but her life-spirit has entered another bear who also lies upon her back in the den, invisible, and sleeping the winter sleep. When the spring comes around again, this bear will again issue forth from the den to be again pursued by the hunters, to be again slain, but again to send to the den her life-spirit, to issue forth yet again, when the sun once more awakens the sleeping earth.

Micmac Indians in traditional costume, photographed about 1865. They are probably Christian Morris and her adopted son, Joe. Mrs. Morris was well known for her outstanding craftwork. The peaked hat is a typical article of costume, as are the beaded and ribbon-trimmed coats worn by both these people. The Micmac were an important Algonquian tribe, who occupied Nova Scotia, Cape Breton, and Prince Edward Islands, as well as the northern parts of New Brunswick.

OPPOSITE *Chief Stickwan, photographed by Miles Brothers about 1902. This man was a leader of the Klutina-Copper band of the Athapaskan-speaking Lower Ahtna in the Copper River valley of Southern Alaska. Chief Stickwan is wearing a shell and bead necklace, particularly popular items among these people. He was probably also a shaman — individuals who had more than average knowledge of the spirit powers and mythological lore of the tribe.*

RIGHT *Two fine looking Ahtna girls who lived in the region of the Copper River Valley, photographed about 1903. Early travellers described the Ahtna as tall, fine-looking people with well kept hair and smooth olive complexions. They often wore nose and ear ornaments of shell or metal, and dentalium shell necklaces with an abalone disc, as worn by the girl on the right, were particularly popular.*

THE SUN AND THE MOON
(*Athapaskan*)

There was once a large village, where there lived a family of four boys, with their younger sister, making five children. And, as the story goes, the girl refused to marry when she grew up, even though many suitors came from a distance as well as from her own village.

And, as she continued to refuse them, by and by the men and women of her set were all married off. At that time, there was no sun and moon, and the earth was in a kind of twilight.

So this woman lived on, though the strangers no longer came, and her own mates took no further notice of her, being married already.

At length, one night, some one came and scratched her head while she was asleep. "There are no strangers in the village," thought she. "Who can this be?" Nevertheless, she spoke with him. Every night this man who spoke with her did the same thing, and finally he became as her husband. "But who can it be," she thought. "Every one in the village is married, except my older brother, and there are no strangers here. I will

tie a feather in his hair, and when they leave the kashime, I will go and see who it is that has his hair tied."
"Come," said she, "leave me and go to the kashime. Come! You must have some sleep, and I am sleepy too."
So she spoke after she had tied the feather in his hair, and he left her and went to the kashime, while she lay awake, thinking.

When it began to grow light, she went out and stood at the door of their house, and saw the men coming out, according to their custom, but none of them had the feather in his hair. Suddenly her older brother rushed out. She looked, and there was the feather. The blood rushed to her face, and everything grew dark; then she was overcome with anger. At daylight she brought in (from her cache) her best parka, a beautiful one which had never been worn. Berries also, and deer-fat she brought, without a word, and did not even answer her mother when she spoke to her.

Then, when she had made the fire, she bathed herself, and attired herself in her beautiful parka and her moccasins (as for a journey). Then she took the frozen food (which she had prepared) and put it into her brother's bowl, and taking her housewife's knife, she reached down within her parka and cut off her breasts and put them upon the frozen food, and thrust an awl into each, and went with it to the kashime.

Inside the door, she straightened herself up. Yonder, on the opposite side of the room, sat her brother. She set the dish down by him. "There is no doubt that it was you who did it," she said; "I thought surely it must be some one else. A pestilence will break out upon all mankind for what you have done."

She left the kashime, and yonder, in the east, she went up in the sky as the sun. Then her brother drew on his parka and moccasins also, but in haste he left off one of them. "My sister has escaped me," he thought and he too, going after her, became the moon.

And we do not look at the sun, because we sympathize with her shame.

Three unidentified hop-pickers of the Ahtna tribe. Photograph taken by Darius Kinsey near Snoquahine, Washington, in 1906.

Passamaquoddy Indians and Father Vermilljou; photograph possibly taken in the period 1860-75. Both men and the boy wear traditional headdresses, the men also have bags with broad beaded bands across the shoulder. The Passamaquoddy, who belonged to the Abenaki confederacy, were Algonquian speakers and formerly occupied much of the present state of Maine.

TALE OF THE NORTHERN LIGHTS
(Abenaki)

Old Chief M'Sartto (Morning Star) had an only son, who was so different from the other boys of the tribe as to be a worry to the old chief. He would not stay and play with the others, but would take his bow and arrows, and leave home for days at a time, always going towards the north. When he came home they would ask, "Where have you been, what have you seen?" but he would say nothing. At last the old chief said to his wife, "The boy must be watched. I will follow him." So next time M'Sartto kept in his path and traveled for a long time. Suddenly his eyes closed and he could not hear; he had a curious feeling, then knew nothing. Eventually his eyes opened in a queer, light country, with no sun, moon or stars, but all lit by this peculiar light. He saw many beings, but all were different from his people. They gathered round and tried to talk to him, but he did not understand their language. M'Sartto did not know where to go nor what to do. He was well treated by this strange tribe; he watched their games and was attracted to a wonderful game of ball he had never seen before; it seemed to turn the light to many colours, and the players all had lights on their heads, and all wore very curious belts, called *Menquan*, or Rainbow belts. In a few days an old man came and spoke to M'Sartto in his own language, and asked him if he knew where he was. The old chief said "No." Then the old man said, "You are in the country of *Wa-ba-ban* (northern lights). I came here many years ago. I was the only one here from the 'lower country,' as we call it; but now there is a boy who comes to visit us every few days." Then M'Sartto asked how the old man had got there, which way he had come. The old man said, "I followed a path called the Spirits' Path, *Ket-à-gus-wowt* (Milky-Way)." "This must be same path that I came on," said the old chief. "Did you have a queer feeling as if you had lost all knowledge when you traveled?" "Yes," said the old man, "I could not see nor hear." Then M'Sartto said,

Mrs. Wallace Lewey and granddaughter. Passamaquoddy, probably photographed about 1932 at Princeton, Maine. The Passamaquoddy spoke a dialect close to that of the adjacent Malecite tribe; a small tribe, their numbers were estimated at about 150 in 1726. By the time this photograph was taken, very few representatives of the tribe remained.

"We did come by the same path. Can you tell me how I can get home again?" "Yes, the chief of Wa-ba-ban will send you home safely." "Well, can you tell me where I can see my boy - the boy that comes here to visit you is mine." Then the old man told M'Sartto, "You will see him playing ball if you watch." Chief M'Sartto was very glad to hear this, and when the man went around the wigwams telling everyone to go and have a game of ball, M'Sartto went also. When the game began he saw many beautiful colours in the play-ground. The old man asked him, "Do you see your boy there?" The old chief said he did: "The one with the brightest light on his head is my son." Then they went to the Chief of Northern Lights, and the old man said, "The chief of the Lower Country wants to go home, and also wants his boy." So the Chief of Northern Lights called his people together to bid goodbye to M'Sartto and his son, and then ordered two *K'che Sipps* (great birds) to carry them home. When they were traveling the Milky-way he felt the same strange way he did when going, and when he came to his senses he found himself near home. His wife was very glad when he returned, for when the boy told her his father was safe she paid no attention as she was afraid M'Sartto was lost.

THE PLEIADES
(Cheyenne)

Southern Cheyenne group – Oivit, Amitsehei and Nakai – photograph taken by D. L. Gill about 1908. Amitsehei wears a beautiful cloth dress embellished with elk teeth or cowrie shells. The Fort Laramie Treaty of 1851 officially recognized the Cheyenne as being in two separate sections, the Northern and Southern groups, which ultimately caused the destruction of their formal, compact organization.

A chief had a fine-looking daughter, who had a great many admirers. At night she was visited by a young man, but did not know who he was. She worried about this, and determined to discover him. She put red paint near her bed. At night he crawled on her bed, wearing a white robe. She put her hand into the paint and then on his back. The next day she told her father to call all the young men to a dance in front of his tent. They all came, and the whole village turned out to see them. She watched all that came, looking for the mark she had made. As she turned, she saw one of her father's dogs, with the mark on his back. This disheartened her, so that she went straight into her tent. This broke up the dance. The next day she went into the woods near the camp, with the dog on a string, and hit him. He finally broke loose. She was very unhappy. Several months later she bore seven pups. She told her mother to kill them, but her mother was

A Southern Cheyenne Indian called Waun and probably photographed by C. M. Bell in 1880. The name Cheyenne was probably derived from the Lakota term for them, Shai-la or 'people of an alien language'. They called themselves Dzitsiistas or 'our people' or possibly 'tall people' and were, in fact among the tallest of the Plains tribes.

kind toward them, and made a little shelter for them. They began to grow, and at night the old dog sometimes came to them. After a time, the woman began to take interest in them, and sometimes played with them. When they were big enough to run, the old dog came and took them away. When the woman went to see them in the morning, they were gone. She saw the large dog's tracks, and several little ones, and followed them a distance. She was sad, and cried. She came back to her mother and said: "Mother make me seven pairs of moccasins. I am going to follow the little ones, searching for them." Her mother made seven pairs of moccasins, and she started out, tracking them all the way. Finally, in the distance, she saw a tent. The youngest one came to her, and said: "Mother, father wants you to go back. We are going home; you cannot come." She said: "No, wherever you go, I go." She took the little one, and carried him to the tent. She entered, and saw a young man, who, however, took no notice of her. He gave her a little meat and drink, which did not grow less, however much she ate. She tied the little pup to her belt with a string. Next morning, she was left alone, and the tent was gone. She followed and again came to them. Four times this happened in the same way; but the fourth time the tracks stopped. She looked up, and there she saw seven pups (*Manootóxtcioo*); they were stars (the Pleiades).

THE STAR MAIDEN
(*Chippewa*)

While walking over the prairies, Algon, a hunter, discovered a circular pathway, worn as if by the tread of many feet, though there were no foot-marks visible outside its bounds. The young hunter, who had never before encountered one of these "fairy rings," was filled with surprise at the discovery, and hid himself in the long grass to see whether an explanation might not be forthcoming. He had not long to wait. In a little while he heard the sound of music so faint and sweet that it surpassed anything he had ever dreamed of. The strains grew fuller and richer, and as they seemed to come from above he turned his eyes toward the sky. Far in the blue he could see a tiny white speck like a floating cloud. Nearer and nearer it came, and the astonished hunter saw that it was no cloud, but a dainty osier car, in which were seated twelve beautiful maidens. The music he had heard was the sound of their voices as they sang strange and magical songs. Descending into the charmed ring, they danced around and around with such exquisite grace and abandon that it was a sheer delight to watch them. But after the first moments of dazzled surprise Algon had eyes only for the youngest of the group, a slight, vivacious creature, so fragile and delicate that it seemed to the stalwart hunter that a breath would blow her away.

He was, indeed, seized with a fierce passion for the dainty sprite, and he speedily decided to spring from the grass and carry her off. But the pretty creatures were too quick for him. The fairy of his choice skillfully eluded his grasp and rushed to the car. The others followed, and in a moment they were soaring up in the air, singing a sweet unearthly song. The disconsolate hunter returned to his lodge, but try as he might he could not get the thought of the Star Maiden out of his head, and next day, long before the hour of the fairies' arrival, he lay in the grass awaiting the sweet sounds that would herald their approach. At length the car appeared. The twelve ethereal beings danced as before. Again, Algon made a desperate attempt to seize the youngest, and again he was unsuccessful.

"Let us stay," said one of the Star Maidens. "Perhaps the mortal wishes to teach us his earthly dances." But the youngest sister would not hear of it, and they all rose out of sight in their osier basket.

Poor Algon returned home more unhappy than ever. All night he lay awake dreaming of the pretty, elusive creature who had wound a chain of gossamer round his heart and brain, and early in the morning he repaired to the enchanted spot. Casting about for some means of gaining his end, he came upon the hollow trunk of a tree in which a number of mice gamboled. With the aid of the charms in his "medicine"-bag he turned himself into one of these little animals, thinking the fair sisters would never pierce his disguise.

That day when the osier car descended its occupants alighted and danced merrily as they were wont in the magic circle, till the youngest saw the hollow tree-trunk (which had not been there on the previous day) and turned to fly. Her sisters laughed at her fears, and tried to reassure her by overturning the tree-trunk. The mice scampered in all directions, and were quickly pursued by the Star Maidens, who killed them all except Algon. The latter regained his own shape just as the youngest fairy raised her hand to strike him. Clasping her in his arms, he bore her to his village, while her frightened sisters ascended to their Star-country.

Arrived at his home, Algon married the maiden, and by his kindness and gentleness soon won her affection. However, her thoughts still dwelt on her own people, and though she indulged her sorrow only in secret, lest it should trouble her husband, she never ceased to lament her lost home.

One day while she was out with her little son she made a basket of osiers, like the one in which she had first come to earth. Gathering together some flowers and gifts for the Star-people, she took the child with her into the basket, sang the magical songs she still remembered, and soon floated up to her own country, where she was welcomed by the king, her father.

Algon's grief was bitter indeed when he found that his wife and child had left him. But he had no means of following them. Every day he would go to the magic circle on the prairie and give vent to his sorrow, but the years went past and there was no sign of his dear ones returning.

Meanwhile the woman and her son had almost forgotten Algon and the earth-country. However, when the boy grew old enough to hear the story he wished to go and see his father. His mother consented, and arranged to go with him. While they were preparing to descend the Star-people said:

"Bring Algon with you when you return and ask him to bring some feature from every beast and bird he has killed in the chase."

Algon, who had latterly spent almost all his time at the charmed circle, was overjoyed to see his wife and son come back to him, and willingly agreed to go with them to the Star-country. He worked very hard to obtain a specimen of all the rare and curious birds and beasts in his land, and when at last he had gathered the relics – a claw of one, a feather of another, and so on – he piled them in the osier car, climbed in himself with his wife and boy, and set off to the Star-country.

The people there were delighted with the curious gifts Algon had brought them, and, being permitted by their king to take one apiece, they did so. Those who took a tail or a claw of any beast at once became the quadruped represented by the fragment, and those who took the wings of birds became birds themselves. Algon and his wife and son took the feathers of a white falcon and flew down to the prairies, where their descendants may still be seen.

Qui-wi-zhen-shish or 'Bad Boy', a Chippewa warrior of the Red Lake Band in Minnesota, photographed prior to 1872, when he died. This man was ranked as one of the bravest of the Chippewas in their battle with the Sioux and took many scalps. He was an eloquent speaker and a man of great influence. In later years, he became a successful farmer. Qui-wi-zhen-shish had two wives.

WAR WITH THE SKY PEOPLE
(*Salishan*)

Once upon a time the people wanted to make war on the Sky people. Grizzly-Bear, who was chief, called all the people together to shoot arrows at the sky. Each animal and bird shot, but all the arrows fell short. The Fish, Snakes, and Toads also tried. At last only Chickadee (or Wren?) was left, and no one expected that he could hit the sky. Coyote said he did not need to try, when he himself had failed. However, Chickadee's arrow hit the sky. The others all shot in turn again, and Chickadee shot an arrow which stuck in the nock of the first one. They kept on shooting until a chain of arrows had been made which reached the ground. On this they climbed to the sky. Grizzly-Bear and Black-Bear only remained. They quarreled as to who should climb next. Black-Bear said Grizzly was too heavy and would break the ladder. They chased each other around the ladder, and finally knocked it down. Meanwhile the people who had reached the sky had attacked the people there, and had been defeated. They fled; and when the first ones reached the hole in the sky, they descended one after another. When they reached half way down, they found the lower part gone, and hesitated to drop so far. Meanwhile the people crowded so thickly on the

A Medicine Man and participant within the Midewiwin or 'Grand Medicine Lodge' of the Chippewa. Photograph taken at Lac Courte, Oreille Reservation, Wisconsin (by A.E. Jenks) in 1899. The spiritual life of the Chippewa was centered around the Midewiwin, the members of which passed through eight degrees of the order by initiation. The various spirits that figured in Chippewa mythology were represented, often as subordinate beings, in the Midewiwin ceremonies.

ladder above, that their weight broke it, and they all fell down. Those left above threw themselves down, and killed or hurt themselves, while the remainder were killed by the Sky people. The Fish, who had no wings, fared worst. Sucker broke all his bones.

TALE OF THE PLEIADES
(*Onondaga*)

A long time ago a party of Indians went through the woods toward a good hunting-ground, which they had long known. They traveled several days through a very wild country, going on leisurely and camping by the way. At last they reached *Kan-ya-ti-yo*, "the beautiful lake," where the gray rocks were crowned with great forest trees. Fish swarmed in the waters, and at every jutting point the deer came down from the hills around to bathe or drink of the lake. On the hills and in the valleys were huge beech and chestnut trees, where squirrels chattered, and bears came to take their morning and evening meals.

A Flathead Dance group probably photographed near Flathead Lake, Western Montana, about 1910. The name of this Salishan-speaking tribe arose not because they artificially deformed the head, but because in contrast to several tribes further west, they left them in their natural condition, that is flat on top. Much of their mythology centered around the powers of animals and the sky.

The chief of the band was Hah-yah-no, "Tracks in the water," and he halted his party on the lake shore that he might return thanks to the Great Spirit for their safe arrival at this good hunting-ground. "Here will we build our lodges for the winter, and may the Great Spirit, who has prospered us on our way, send us plenty of game, and health and peace." The Indian is always thankful.

The pleasant autumn days passed on. The lodges had been built, and hunting had prospered, when the children took a fancy to dance for their own amusement. They were getting lonesome, having little to do, and so they met daily in a quiet spot by the lake to have what they called their jolly dance. They had done this a long time, when one day a very old man came to them. They had seen no one like him before. He was dressed in white feathers, and his white hair shone like silver. If his appearance was strange, his words were unpleasant as well. He told them they must stop their dancing, or evil would happen to them. Little did the children heed, for they were intent on their sport, and again and again the old man appeared, repeating his warning.

The mere dances did not afford all the enjoyment the children wished, and a little boy, who like a good dinner, suggested a feast the next time they met. The food must come from their parents, and all these were asked when they returned home. "You will waste and spoil good victuals," said one, "You can eat at home as

91

you should," said another, and so they got nothing at all. Sorry as they were for this, they met and danced as before. A little to eat after each dance would have made them happy indeed. Empty stomachs cause no joy.

One day, as they danced, they found themselves rising little by little into the air, their heads being light through hunger. How this happened they did not know, but one said, "Do not look back, for something strange is taking place." A woman, too, saw them rise, and called them back, but with no effect, for they still rose slowly above the earth. She ran to the camp. and all rushed out with food of every kind, but the children would not return, though their parents called piteously after them. But one would even look back, and he became a falling star. The others reached the sky, and are now what we call the Pleiades, and the Onondagas Oot-kwa-tab. Every falling or shooting star recalls the story, but the seven stars shine on continuously, a pretty band of dancing children.

THIS PAGE *A Mohawk boy wearing elements of traditional clothing, photographed on the Caughnawaga Reserve in Quebec, Canada, prior to March 1914. The Caughnawaga Reserve was of mixed Oneida and Mohawk descent but, for all practical purposes, today it is considered Mohawk. Note the traditional assumption sash around the boy's waist, which, embellished in a certain way, designated rank.*

OPPOSITE *William Henry Fishcarrier, a Cayuga (Iroquoian), full-blood head chief. His Cayuga name was Ho-jah-ge-teh, 'Fishcarrier'; note the floral beaded band on his shoulder, a style typical for the mid to late nineteenth century, as is roached hair. The Cayuga had ten delegates in the Five Nations of the Iroquois and formerly occupied the shores of Cayuga Lake in present-day New York State.*

—4—

Gods and Goddesses

OST OF THE CULTURAL AREAS make reference to a supreme being who had always existed and who created primordial lifeforms or gave the task to lesser deities.

Such powers were referred to as Manitou (Algonquian), Wakanda (Siouan), Orenda (Iroquoian) and Sulia (Salishan), all referring to a mysterious potency far superior to the natural abilities of earth bound man. Within the cultural areas, there were certain linguistic variations – thus, the myth of Menabozho (p. 98) of the Chippewa, clearly refers to Manitou who in other myths of the Algonquians appears as a great hare called Michabo, who was credited with creating the world and was the ruler of the winds. His other great achievements were the Sky Powers of picture writing and inventing the fishing net.[6]

For the Pawnee, it was Tirawahat who was ever present in all things and the great blue dome of the sky was strongly associated with this mysterious power. The first thunder of the spring was viewed as communication through the lesser deity, Paruksti, who acted as a messenger to Tirawahat and used thunder as his speech – initiating the complex Pawnee ceremonies relating to renewal and growth. Gods associated with thunder were widely distributed in North America, thus the Cherokee Thunder God was Asgaya Gigei, red in colour and said to typify lightning; he was described as the keeper of all the game in Cherokee territory and had to be propitiated before and after the hunt.

The awesome power of the Thunderbird figures prominently in the mythology of the Northwest Coast tribes. Referred to as Hagwelawremrhskyoek or 'Sea-monster Eagle' by the coastal Tsimshian, this giant bird was said to swoop from the sky and devour whales. The blinking of its eyes created a lightning flash and the flapping of its great wings produced thunder. In the Coast Salish Thunderbird Dance, 'a small amount of gunpowder was ignited near the ceremonial house entrance to represent the flash of his eyes' (Barnett p. 296, also in Sheehan, p. 87).

The voice of the Thunder god Wakinyan was said to reverberate through the hills and badlands in Lakota (Plains) territory. Sometimes a symbol of the awesome power of lightning, described as being due to the flashing of his eyes, was rendered on costume or war accoutrements in the form of a zigzag line, indicative of direct communication with this deity. In Lakota mythology, the war horse was linked to Wakinyan undoubtedly as a wish, a plea, that the creature would enable the same death-dealing qualities of the lightning to be bestowed on its owner [7] (Wissler, p. 46). The tale of the Sky God (p. 117) underlines the Hopi tribe's concern with the great powers of nature, especially those of storm, thunder, lightning, and rain, many of which were personified in Kachinas, which were endowed with magical powers.

Awonawilona, 'The Creator', of the Zuni, has been described as one of the most perfect examples of a deity 'in its constructive aspect to be found in the mythologies of America' (Spence, 1916, p. 121). Identified with the sun, he was spoken of as the architect of the universe although he seemed to lack close touch with mankind. Lesser deities, such as the Zuni salt goddess (p. 101), were more firmly associated with human beings and because she was said to be the producer of salt – which appeared at the edges of pools in Zuni territory – brought wealth to the tribe, who traded this commodity to more distant peoples. The salt goddess also displayed human characteristics – she fell in love with and married the god of turquoise, a semi-precious stone much used by the Indians of the Southwest as a decorative material.

A debate regarding the existence of God is part of the subject of the Huron myth relating to the sorcerer, Tijaiha (p. 103) who made a contract with an underwater serpent sacrificing his mother-in-law to acquire power that would allow him to destroy his enemies. The missionaries attempted to convert the Huron to Christianity, emphasizing that there was only one God, but the Indians refused to accept its truth. Finally, the priests accepted the Hurons' belief that there were two Gods – the Holy Ghost and Jesus – and suggested that one of these might be the same as the Indian god. In this respect, they were more successful than a certain Father Rogel who, in 1570, told the tribes who lived near the Savannah river, that the deity they revered was a demon who loved all evil things and that they must hate him. It is reliably reported that the Indians 'indignantly left the missionary to preach to the winds' (Spence, 1916, p. 105).

The Cheyennes' (Plains) search for the new Christ is the subject of 'About the Messiah' (p. 106) relating to the Ghost Dance religion which, originating among the Paiutes at Walker Lake in Utah, swept the Plains in the 1890's. Here, ancient mythological concepts were intertwined with Christianity, the leader suggesting

PREVIOUS PAGE *Carved wooden effigies of the Elder God of War from the shrine on the Twin Mountains near the Pueblo of Zuni, New Mexico. (Originally published in the 23rd Annual Report of the Bureau of American Ethnology, 1893.) Photographed by Stevenson prior to 1893. There were numerous shrines on the sacred mesa of the Zuni, called Taaiyalone, perhaps among the most important was that of the Twin War Gods of the Zuni.*

that a God of the Indians would sweep away the white invaders from their homelands. In the mythology of the Ghost Dance, the Messiah was to come to restore the earthand its happy past to his red children. He would abolish their major problems – disease, decimation, loss of old ways, and the white man. The symbol for the Messiah was the Morning Star and as the song below indicates, we can account for the frequent use of this symbol on Ghost Dance clothing (Eppridge, p. 44).

> Father, the Morning Star!
> Father, the Morning Star!
> Look on us, we have danced until daylight,
> Look on us, we have danced until daylight.
> Take pity on us ... Hi'i'i'!
> Take pity on us ... Hi'i'i'!

(Mooney, 1896, p. 1011)

The Navajo war gods, Nayenezgani and To'badzistsini are the subject of The Black God myth (p. 110). In this story, Hastsézini, the Black God, after much wrangling, is persuaded by a messenger from the Navajoes to cure the war gods from the diseases in many parts of their bodies, which crippled their fighting powers. The myth refers to the production of an infusion composed of various ingredients, and the use of feathers, charcoal, bracelets of yucca leaves and sacred strings, all of which were used to cure the war gods of their ailments. The myth thus touches on the origin of medicine as a gift from the higher powers and refers to the many materials that were used to evoke help in Navajo ceremonies and rituals.

MENABOZHO
(Chippewa)

Menabozho, the great land manitou, did not like the water manitous or spirits. One day he saw the chief of the water manitous asleep on a rock, and he shot and killed him with a magic arrow, then the little water manitous called the big rivers to help them and chased Menabozho up a high hill.

The water reached halfway up the hill; the water manitous then called all the little rivers to help them. The water chased Menabozho to the top of the high hill. He climbed up a tall pine tree, but the water came up to his chin; it could not go over his head, for there is not water enough in the whole world to drown the great Menabozho.

He waited a long time while he stood on the top of the pine tree. The rivers would not go back, and he could not see any land.

A loon flew over his head and then dived into the great water. Menabozho said: "Brother Loon, come to me. I must make land for us to stand on. Will you dive down and bring me a little sand?"

The loon put down his head and went through the deep water, but it was too deep even for the great loon-bird. He came up again, but he had left his breath in the deep water. Menabozho caught him as he floated by the pine tree, but he found no sand in his bill nor on his feet.

An otter put his head out of the water close by Menabozho.

"Brother Otter, dive down and bring me up a few grains of sand. We must have land to put our feet upon.

The otter knew he must do as Menabozho told him, so he put his head down into the deep water. He came up, but he had no life any more, and Menabozho could not find any sand in his paws.

A pair of child's moccasins, Chippewa, circa 1890. The moccasins are made of white buckskin and have soft soles with beadwork on a black cloth background and red braid edges and ties; both sinew and trade thread have been used in their manufacture.

Medicine Man's conjuring lodge – frame set up at the Grand Medicine Society Dance at Lac Courte, Oreille Reservation, Wisconsin in 1899. This photograph is by A. E. Jenks who reported that he saw this frame made during the dance for a candidate who was taken sick. The frame was covered with hides or canvas, and by clever (and secret) cord attachments to the flimsy frame, the Medicine Man inside made the tent sway from side to side, enhancing the drama of the occasion as he communicated with the higher powers.

A muskrat came swimming by just then. "Brother Muskrat, you are very brave. Will you dive down to the sand under this deep water and bring me a few grains? I must make land for my brothers," said Menabozho.

The muskrat was brave, for he dived down, but he came up just like the otter. He had no more life, but he had a little sand in one front paw.

Menabozho held the sand in his own hand and dried it in the sunshine. He blew it with his breath far out on the water, and it made a little island. Menabozho called the sand back to him. He dried it in his hand again and then blew it to its place on the deep water. He did this for two days, and the island grew larger every time it was sent back. Menabozho left the tree and walked on the land.

He called to his brothers, who are the trees, animals, and everything on the land, to come and live on this land. The water had to go back to its place.

GODDESS OF SALT
(*Zuni*)

B etween Zuni and Pescado is a steep mesa, or table-land, with fantastic rocks weathered into tower- and roof-like prominences on its sides, while near it is a high natural monument of stone. Say the Zunis: the goddess of salt was so troubled by the people who lived near her domain on the sea-shore, and who took away her snowy treasures without offering any sacrifice in return, that she forsook the ocean and went to live in the mountains far away. Whenever she stopped beside a pool to rest she made it salt, and she wandered so long about the great basins of the West that much of the water in them is bitter, and the yield of salt from the larger lake near Zuni brings into the Zuni treasury large tolls from other tribes that draw from it.

Here she met the turquoise god, who fell in love with her at sight, and wooed so warmly that she accepted and married him. For a time they lived happily, but when the people learned that the goddess had concealed herself among the mountains of New Mexico they followed her to that land and troubled her again until she declared that she would leave their view forever. She entered this mesa, breaking her way through a high wall of sandstone as she did so. The arched portal through which she passed is plainly visible. As she went through, one of her plumes was broken off, and falling into the valley it tipped upon its stem and became the monument that is seen there. The god of turquoise followed his wife, and his footsteps may be traced in outcrops of pale-blue stone.

Left half of a panoramic view of the volcanic crater, 60 miles south of the Pueblo of Zuni in New Mexico. Photograph by Mindeleff prior to 1898. This is a lake from which the Zuni and other tribes procure salt, which is considered to be of high quality and a valuable trade item. The Zuni goddess, Mawe or 'Salt Mother' is credited with bringing salt to the tribe. Such sources are considered sacred and now only accessible to privileged individuals.

Wewa, a Zuni male transvestite spinning wool. Photograph probably taken by John Hillers about 1885. This person's hair is cut in a woman's style and typical female attire is worn, such as a woven sash and belt and cotton blouse. Such people often excelled at craftwork and were generally socially accepted – even among such tribes as the war-like Plains Indians

Designs in moosehair embroidery worked on a birch bark box, probably Lorette Huron, circa 1860. Traditional costume is shown on the human figure – a shirt with sash and red leggings with knee garters. Much encouraged by missionaries, the Huron produced such work to supplement their income. Moosehair embroidery was an ancient craft in the Northeast cultural area.

THE STORY OF TIJAIHA, THE SORCERER
(*Huron*)

When the French came the missionaries tried to prevail on the Indians to receive their religion. They asked the Indians if they knew anything about God. The Indians replied that they did: that three or four times a year they had meetings, at which the women and children were present, and then the chiefs told them what to do and warned them against evil practices. The missionaries said that this was good, but that there was a better way, which they ought know. They ought to become Christians. But the Indians said, "We have many friends among the creatures about us. Some of us have snake friends, some eagles, some bears, and the like. How can we desert our friends?" The priests replied, "There is only one God." "No," said the Indians, "there are two gods, one for the Indians and the other for the whites." The discussion lasted three days. Finally, the priests said it was true – there were two Gods, Jesus and the Holy Ghost. One of these might be the same as the Indian God. The Indians could follow all his commands which were good, and also obey the commands of Jesus. But they would have to give up their allies among the brutes.

Some of the Hurons became Christians, but others refused to accept the new religion. Among these was a noted warrior, a young man, named Tijaiha. On one occasion he left the town with his family to hunt on the Huron River. One day, coming to a deep pool near the river, he beheld a violent commotion in the water, which was evidently made by a living creature. Of what nature it might be he did not know, though he believed it to be a great serpent, and to be possessed, like many of the wild creatures, of supernatural powers. Thereupon, after the fashion of the Indians, he fasted for ten days, eating occasionally only a few morsels to preserve life; and he prayed to the creature that some of its power might be bestowed on him. At the end of the tenth day a voice from the disturbed pool demanded what he wanted. He replied that he wanted to have such power given to him that he could vanquish and destroy all his enemies. She (the creature) replied that this power should be conferred upon him if he would grant her what she desired. He asked what this was, and was told that she would require one of his children. If he would grant this demand, he might come at night and learn from her the secret which would give him the power he sought for. He objected to this sacrifice, but offered, in place of the child, to give an old woman, his wife's mother. The creature accepted the substitute, and the bargain was concluded.

That night Tijaiha returned to the pool, and learned what he had to do. He was to prepare a cedar arrow, with which he must shoot the creature when she should appear, at his call, above the water. From the wound he could then draw a small quantity of blood, the possession of which would render him invincible, and enable him to destroy his enemies. But as this blood was a deadly poison, and even its effluvia might be mortal, he must prepare an antidote from the juice of a plant which she named. On the following day he procured the plant, and his wife – who knew nothing of the fatal price he was to pay – assisted him in making the infusion. He also made a cedar arrow, and, with bow in hand, repaired to the pool.

At his call the water began to rise, boiling fearfully. As it rose, an animal came forth. It proved to be a large bird, a "diver," and the warrior said, "This is not the one," and let it go. The water boiled and rose higher, and a porcupine came out. "Neither is this the one," said the warrior, and withdrew his arrow from his bow. Then the water rose in fury to the level of the bank, and the head of a huge horned serpent, with distended jaws and flaming eyes, rose and glared at Tijaiha. "This is the one," he said, and shot the creature in the neck. The blood gushed forth, and he caught, in a vessel which he held ready, about half a pint. Then he ran toward his lodge, but before he reached it he had become nearly blind and all but helpless. His wife put the kettle to his lips. He drank the antidote, and presently vomited the black poison, and regained his strength. In the morning he called to his wife's mother, but she was dead. She had perished without a touch from a human hand. In this manner he became possessed of a talisman which, as he believed, would give him a charmed life, and secure him the victory over his enemies.

But in some way it became known that he had been the cause of the mother's death. This crime excited the indignation of his people, and he dared not go back to them. He took refuge with the Iroquois, and became a noted war-chief among them. After some time he resolved, in an evil hour, to lead an attack against his own people. He set forth at the head of a strong party of warriors, and arrived at the Wyandot settlement, near the present town of Sandwich. It was the season of corn-planting, and two of Tijaiha's aunts had come out on that day to plant their fields. They were women of high rank in the tribe, and Tijaiha knew that their death would arouse the whole tribe. He ordered his followers to kill them. This they did, and then retreated into the forest to the northward, carefully covering their tracks, to escape pursuit. Their leader's expectation was that the Huron warriors would go off in another direction in search of their enemies, thus leaving their defenceless town at his mercy.

When the Hurons found the bodies they were greatly excited. They searched for ten days without discovering any trace of the murderers. Their chief then consulted a noted soothsayer, who promised that on the following day he would tell him all. During the night the soothsayer made his incantations, and in the

Three generations of the Francois family, Huron. Photograph by Notman, circa 1900. The Huron were a confederation of four highly organized Iroquoian tribes, who, when first known in 1615, occupied a territory sometimes referred to as Huronia, near Georgian Bay, Ontario. They were at almost continuous war with the Iroquois.

Matthew Mudeater, a Huron chief. He was a delegate to Washington, DC, in 1875. By this time all remnants of traditional costume had virtually vanished, but the spirit of a proud race is written in the features of this chief. Many Huron were adopted by the Iroquois after their repeated defeats by this tribe in the 17th and 18th centuries.

morning informed the Hurons that the deed had been done by a party of Iroquois, under the lead of Tijaiha. The enemy, he said, was lurking in the woods, and he could guide them to the spot, but they must wait ten days before starting. The Hurons waited impatiently until the ten days had expired, and then placed the old soothsayer on horseback, and followed him. He led them through the forest directly to the encampment of their enemies. On seeing them they waited till evening, and then through the night, till daybreak. Then, according to their custom, they shouted to their sleeping foes, and rushed upon them. They killed every man in the camp; but on examining carefully the bodies, they were annoyed to find that Tijaiha was not among them.

Being hungry, they seated themselves to eat, and the chief, feeling thirsty, told his son to take his kettle and bring some water. "Where shall I find water here?" asked the boy. "These men must have had water," replied his father. "Look for the path they have made to it." The lad looked, and found the path, and, following it, came to a deep spring or pool under a tree. As he was stooping down to it a man rose partly out of the pool, and bade the youth take him prisoner. The frightened boy ran to the camp and told what he had seen. All shouted "Tijaiha," and rushed to the pool, where they dragged him forth by the hair. He stood defiant and sneering, while they attempted to kill him. Their blows seemed powerless to injure him. He caught the tomahawks which were aimed at him, and hurled them back. At length a warrior, exclaiming, "I will finish him," plunged a knife into his breast and tore out his heart. Thrown on the ground, it bounded like a living thing, till the warrior split it open with his knife. Thus ended Tijaiha's evil career. His contract with the serpent had only led him to crime and death.

ABOUT THE MESSIAH
(Cheyenne)

Dear Friends – one and all. Don't force your and others' minds on this letter, but resist it and keep your minds from it. I simply want to tell you just what I learned from Mr. Porcupine, Big Beaver, and I am sorry to say from one of them, a cousin of mine, Ridge Walker, son of Beaver Claws. I expect many of you are wishing to know, and perhaps many of you have already heard about it. I have met them face to face, and have questioned them personally when I met them; and so I learned from them some of their Messiah ideas. I shall try to make an account of just what I have learned from these three persons.

In the fall of the year 1890, they say, they first heard of this new Christ, at the Arapaho and Shoshone Agency, Wyoming Territory. When they and other Cheyennes of Tongue River went on a visit to the said tribes in the autumn of 1890, an Arapaho Indian named Sage, who had been to the southwestern country in 1888, told them that a new Christ had arisen for the Indians; he said where he could be found and explained his doctrine to them. Farther on, Porcupine said that he and the other Cheyennes were much interested, and determined to see the Messiah, but as all could not go so far, nine of these Cheyennes were sent back to

LEFT Skki-hi-una *or 'Little Hand', a southern Cheyenne aged 59, photographed by D. I. Gill in 1909. The man lived at Cantoment, Western Oklahoma, where the Southern Cheyenne were given a reservation in 1867, although they refused to settle there until a formal surrender was made in 1875. In 1904, they numbered just under 2,000.*

OPPOSITE Hapei, *a Southern Cheyenne woman and wife of Charles Murphy. Photographed in 1908 at the age of 33 by D. L. Gill at Cantonment, western Oklahoma. She wears heavy rows of beads around her neck and a trade blanket – probably obtained from the Southwestern tribes – around her shoulders*

Ridge Walker, a Northern Cheyenne scout, photographed between 1888 and 1897 at Fort Keogh, Montana, probably by Christian Barthelmess. When the Ghost Dance swept the Plains in the 1890s (see p. 106), Ridge Walker visited its originator Wovoka, to establish the true doctrine of the new religion.

Tongue River Agency to tell the people what they had heard. Porcupine and several of the Cheyennes went on. When they arrived in Utah, they received large accessions to their caravan. Indians joining them *en route* at the different points, and so at last their meeting took place at Walker Lake to hear the new Christ speak. There were many people present, including women and children.

Then Mr. Porcupine says to the Messiah: "I and my people have been living in ignorance until I went and found out the truth." He sat with his head bowed all the time, and after a while he arose and said he was very glad to see his children: "I have sent for you and I am glad that you have come, and I am going to talk to you after a while about our relations who are dead and gone. My children, I want you to listen to all I have to say, and I will teach you how to dance a dance, and I want you to dance it; get ready for the dance, and then when the dance is over I will talk to you."

He was dressed in a white coat with stripes; the rest of his dress was that of a white man's, except that he had a pair of moccasins. And then we commenced to dance, everybody joining in with the Christ, singing while we danced. We danced till late in the night, and he said we had danced enough. And in the morning after breakfast we went in the circle and spread grass over it on the ground, the Christ standing in the midst of us, and told us that he was going away on that day and that he would be back next morning and talk to us.

In the night, when I first saw him I thought he was an Indian; but the next day, when I could see him better, he looked different; he was not so dark as an Indian, nor so light as a white man. He had no beard or whiskers, but very heavy eye-brows: he was a good-looking man, and we were crowded up very close.

We had been told that nobody was to talk: and even if a thing was whispered, the Christ would know it. I heard that Christ had been crucified, and I looked to see and I saw a scar on his wrist and one on his face and he seemed to be the man. I could not see his feet.

He would talk to us all day. On that evening we were all assembled again to part with him. When we assembled he began to sing, and he commenced to tremble all over violently for a while, and then sat down; and we danced all on that night, the Christ lying beside us apparently dead. The next morning we went to our breakfast; the Christ was with us again. After breakfast four heralds went around and called out that the Christ was back with us, and wanted to talk with us; and so the circle was made again; they assembled and Christ came amongst them and sat down. He said they were to listen to him while he talked to us. "I am the man who made everything you see around you. I am not lying to my children. I made this earth and everything on it. I have been to Heaven and seen your dead friends, and seen my father and mother. In the beginning, after God made the earth, they sent me back to teach the people; and when I came back to earth, the people were afraid of me and treated me badly. This is what they have done to me (showing his scars). I did not try to defend myself, and I found my children were bad, so I went back to Heaven and left them; and in so many years I would come back and see to my children, and at the end of this time I was sent back to teach them. My father told me that the earth is getting old and worn out, and that the people were getting bad, and that I was to renew everything as it used to be, and make it better, and he said all our dead were to be resurrected and they were all to come back to the earth, and that the earth was too small for them and us; he would do away with heaven and make the earth large enough to contain us all; and that we must tell all the people we meet about these things.

He spoke to us about fighting, and said that was bad and we must keep from it; that the earth was to be all good hereafter; that we must be friends with one another. He said that in the fall of the year the youth of all the good people would be renewed, so that nobody would be more than forty years old. The youth of every one would be renewed in the spring. He said if we were all good he would send people among us who could heal all our wounds and sickness by mere touch, and that we could live forever.

This is what I have witnessed, and many other things wonderful which I cannot describe. Please don't follow the ideas of that man. He is not the Christ. No man in the world can see God at any time. Even the angels of God cannot.

THE BLACK GOD
(*Navajo*)

I t is long since the Navajoes went to war; but in former days when they fought their enemies they often
suffered from war diseases. Their young men know nothing of this. One who killed an enemy by striking
him in the chest would get disease in the chest; one who killed his enemy by striking him on the head would
get disease of the head, and one who killed by wounding in the abdomen would get disease of that part.

Thus it came to pass that, in the ancient days, when the war-gods Nayénezgani and To'badzistsini had
killed many of the Alien Gods, they got war diseases in many parts of their bodies. They suffered much and
became so weak that they could not walk. Their friends tried all the remedies they could think of, but for a
long time no cure was found.

At length some one said: "There is one dwelling at Tse'zindiai (Black Standing Rock) named Dóntso
(an insect) who knows of one who can cure war disease." So the people lay in wait for Dóntso and caught
him. "Who is it that can cure the war disease?" they asked. "I dare not tell," said Dóntso; "it is one whom I
fear, who does not like to have his power known," But the people persisted and persuaded and threatened till
at last Dóntso said: "It is Hastsézini (Black God), the owner of all fire. But never let him know it was I who
revealed the secret, for I fear his vengeance."

A Navajo woman and child. The term 'Na'-va-ho' is from the Tewa language, which is found across a large area of cultivated lands. An Athapaskan speaking tribe, they were referred to by the Spaniards as 'Apaches de Navajo'. This woman wears silver and turquoise jewelry typical of the tribe from the late nineteenth century onwards.

ABOVE *Navajo camp scene showing a typical Navajo habitation referred to by whites as a hogan. At the left is Pesh-lakai-ilhni, a skilled silversmith working the silver on a metal anvil; at the right a man is using a pump drill to drill turquoise. Pesh-lakai-ilhni's son holds bellows, which were used in the smelting of the silver.*

RIGHT *A fine Navajo silver and turquoise necklace, circa 1910. This is a typical 'squash blossom' necklace of the period. The technique of silverwork was learned from the Spanish, the Navajo combining trade silver with the semi-precious turquoise that was commonly found in their traditional territory of Arizona and New Mexico.*

On hearing this, the people got a sacred buckskin, filled it with jeweled baskets, precious stones, shells, feathers, and all the treasures the gods most prize, and sent the bundle by a messenger to Hastsézini. When the messenger entered the house of the fire-god, he found the latter lying on the ground with his back to the fire – a favorite attitude of his. The messenger presented his bundle and delivered his message; but the fire-god only said, "Begone! Go home and take your bundle with you."

The messenger returned to his people and told the result of his errand. They filled another sacred buckskin with precious things and sent him back with two bundles as a present to Black God; but the latter never rose from the ground or took his back from the fire. He dismissed the messenger again with angry words. Once more the messenger was sent back with three bundles and again with four bundles of goods tied up in sacred buckskins; but the god only bade him begone, as he had done before. When he returned to his people he found them singing.

Now Dóntso appeared before them and asked them what they had offered the fire-god. They told him, and added: "We have offered him great pay for his medicine, but he refuses to aid us, and sends our messenger away with angry words." "He is not like other gods," said Dóntso; "he is surly and exclusive. Few of the holy ones ever visit him, and he rarely visits any one. He cares nothing for your sacred buckskins, your baskets of turquoise and white shell, your abalone and rock crystal. All he wants is a smoke, but his cigarette must be made in a very particular way." And then he told them how to make the cigarette sacred to Hastsézini. But he made the people all pledge secrecy. He lived with the fire-god, and thus he came to know how the cigarette should be made and how it should be given to the god.

Three messengers now went to Hastsézini. Two remained outside, and one went in to deliver the cigarette, and thus he gave it: He carried it from the right foot of the god, up along his body, over his forehead, down his left side, and laid it on his left instep. Shading his eyes with his hand, the god gazed at the cigarette on his instep. He picked it up, examined it on all sides, and said angrily: "Who taught you to

'Emerging from the Sweat', Navajo photographed by Edward S. Curtis in 1905. This is part of the Yeibichai or Night Chant ceremony led by two masked men with body paint and in the costume of the Haashcheettii or Talking God. Nearby is the female god (Haashcheeh Ba'aad). This is one of the many Navajo ceremonies for curing sickness, here the patient is surrounded by a circle of prayer sticks.

make this cigarette? No one knows how to make it but Hastíniazi (Little Old Man) and Dóntso. One of these must have taught you." The messenger replied: "I made it myself according to my own thoughts. No one taught me. Dóntso dwells above you and watches you day and night, he never leaves you." Hastsézini examined the cigarette again, inhaled its odor four times, and said: "Láa! It is well! This is my cigarette. Stay you and show me the way I must travel. Let the other messengers go home in advance. I shall get there on the morning of the third day." But they begged him to start that night. He bade the messengers who went in advance to kill a deer with two prongs on each horn, and to boil it all for a feast. When they returned to their home, they told what Hastsézini had said to them, and the people got all things ready as he had directed.

Next morning the Black God left his home, went about half way to Nayénezgani's house, and camped for the night. Many people came to his camp and held a dance there. There were birds among them, for in those days birds were people. And because of this occurrence now, in our day, when Hastsézini camps at night on his way to the medicine-lodge, the people go to his camp and hold a dance.

On the morning after this dance, all left for the house of sickness and got there at sunset. Before they arrived they began to shout and to whoop. The Navajoes in these days shout and whoop, and they call this shouting altsitse. A party from Nayénezgani's house, when they heard the shouting, went out to meet the returning party, and they had a mock battle, in which Hastsézini's party seemed victorious. Such a mock battle is held today in the rites.

When Hastsézini and his party arrived at the lodge there was a feast of the venison. Then the ailing gods said they wished to go out of the lodge. Previously, for many days they had to be carried out; but now they were only helped to rise, and they walked out unaided. The people who came with Hastsézini now went out and began to sing. The Black God was there; he had not yet entered the lodge. But when the people came out he joined them, and when they returned to the lodge he entered with them.

They now burned materials and made two kinds of mixed charcoal. The first was made of pine bark and willow. The second was composed of five ingredients, namely tsildilgisi (a composite plant, Guitierrezzia euthamiae), tlo'nastázi (a gramagrass, Bouteloua birsuta), tsé'aze, or rock-medicine (undetermined), a feather dropped from a live crow, and a feather dropped from a live buzzard. They made four bracelets for the patients, each out of three small yucca leaves plaited together. Then they prepared for each seven sacred strings called wolthád, such as are now used by the shamans, and are so tied to a part that with a single pull they came loose. They pounded together cedar leaves and a plant called thágiitsin and made of these a cold infusion. All present drank of this infusion, and the patients washed their bodies with a portion of it. They applied the wolthád to different parts of the patients' bodies, proceeding from below upwards, viz: feet, knees, hands, and head. While they were tying these, the Black God entered and song was begun. When the singing was half done, the patients and all present drank again of the cold infusion, and the patients washed their bodies with the residue. Assistants next touched each of the ailing gods with black paint made of the second charcoal, on the soles, the palms, on each side of the chest, on each side of the back, over the shoulder-blade, and painted the throat. They greased the bodies of the gods with a big lump of sacred fat, and over this coating of grease they rubbed the first charcoal until the bodies looked as black as that of Hastsézini himself. But they painted the faces with grease and red ochre, and they spotted each cheek in three places with specular iron ore. They put on each a garment called kataha bástsé (worn diagonally like a sash); they tied on the yucca bracelets, and tied a downy eagle feather, plucked from a live eagle, to each head. The two who painted the patients got for a fee four buckskins each. They placed gopher manure in the moccasins of the ailing gods, and then put the moccasins on. They put strings of beads around their necks. They gave to each a bag of medicine, out of the mouth of which stuck the bill of a crow. They began to sing, and sent the tantési (patients) forth from the lodge.

The patients went to a place where lay the scalp of an enemy on which ashes had been sprinkled. Each picked the scalp four times with the crow's bill from his medicine-bag. Then they went to a distance from the lodge and "inhaled the sun." They did not then return to the medicine-lodge, but each went, as he was

FOLLOWING PAGES *The Hopi's* Powamu. *This complex ceremony commences in January or February; the masked dancers or* kachinas *are seen here in the Plaza at the Walpi Pueblo, Arizona. Here, the* kachinas *are dressed as ogres who go from house to house during the ceremony to scare children into obedience to their parents. At the left leading the procession, is Habaiwuhti, a mythical mother of the* kachinas.

instructed, to his home, where a mixture of *gles* (white earth) and water was already prepared for him. Each dipped his hand into this, and marked on the shins, thighs, and other parts of his body the impress of his open hand in white. They partook of corn pollen, the first food they had eaten during the day, and they arose and walked around, happily restored. It was beautiful above them, It was beautiful below them. It was beautiful before them. It was beautiful behind them. It was beautiful all around them.

At sundown Hastsézini left for his home, and the war-gods went back to the medicine-lodge. The people sang all night, and beat the basket-drum. As was done to the gods then, so would they do today, if one among them got the war disease.

PERSONATION OF A SKY GOD WIELDING LIGHTNING
(*Hopi*)

There is an instructive act in the great mystery-play of the Hopi, called the *Palülükoñti*, which gives an idea of the symbolism of form of Sun-god personation, as well as that of the lightning. In this act a masked man representing Shalako stands in the middle of the kiva before the spectators holding an effigy of the Plumed Snake which he causes to coil about his body and head and to dart into the air. The means by which the movement is effected is at first not apparent, but closer examination reveals a false arm hanging at the actor's side in place of his real arm which is inserted in the body of the effigy imparting to it its deceptive movements.

This act represents the Sky-god wielding the lightning, the former represented as Shalako, the latter as the Plumed Snake.

In another episode of this remarkable mystery-play effigies of the Great Serpent are thrust through openings closed by disks with Sun symbols. These effigies are made to knock over a symbolic cornfield. The serpent effigies represent the lightning and the rains and winds which accompany it. They are made to emerge from the Sun symbols representing the Sky-god, whose servants they are or from whom their power comes. They knock over the hills of corn, representing how the floods and winds destroy the works of the farmer. The final part of this episode is also dramatic and symbolic; a man personating the Earth-goddess Hahaiwüqti, wife of the Sky-god, symbolically prays to the angry serpents, symbols of his power – in other words, prays to the god to cease afflicting man and destroying the fields of the farmers by means of his agent the lightning. In both these acts the personation of the lightning is controlled by the Sun or Sky-god; the lightning, once regarded an attribute, has become a special personation controlled by the Sky-god.

Now this Great Serpent conception or personation of lightning has powers which naturally grew up in the mind from analogical reasoning. Certain kinds of rain accompany the lightning; therefore, reasons primitive man, one causes the other, the lightning causes rain, or, to put in another way, the Great Serpent brings the rain. Hence the Sky-god through his agent is a powerful rain-god and symbols of the lightning in form of zigzag designs are constant on Hopi rain altars.

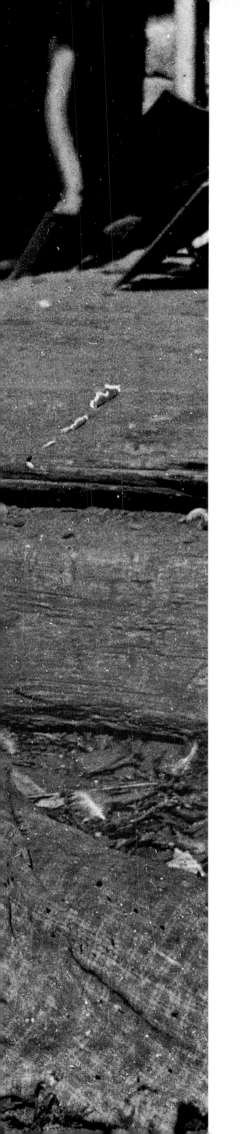

Legends of the Tribes

MANY MYTHS AND LEGENDS of the North American Indians refer to animals and sites that were dominant or characteristic of a particular area. Generally, these oral traditions detail the supernatural powers and ethos of animals, which were viewed as particularly clever and whose attributes were both admired and desired, or they refer to the abode of such powers in places that were designated as sacred and became sites of pilgrimage or sources of inspiration. A Chippewa myth (p. 122) that describes a world in continual darkness, without light or water, tells of the help received from the animals, in particular muskrat, who in an unguarded moment, dropped a burning coal and thus brought fire and light to the world, which then melted the ice, producing water. The peculiar markings of the muskrat are said to be where be burnt himself when carrying the coal.

Generally dominant, however, among these animals were the coyote and the raven although other creatures such as the beaver, fox, blue jay, and even the spider, also figure in many mythological tales. In the Flathead (Plateau) story of how Coyote kills the giant (p. 124), there are references to several of the key characteristics often associated with this creature – his adventurous travelling, cleverness, and strength, as well as his recklessness and zest for tackling the impossible. Among the Nez Perce, another Plateau tribe, Coyote is credited with their very creation. In one version of this legend a monster kills all the animals except Coyote who, furious at the loss of all his friends, climbs a high mountain, ties himself to its peak and challenges the monster to eat him. Coyote proves too clever for the monster and they become friends; later, however, Coyote requests the monster swallow him so that he could see his friends. Once inside its stomach, he stabs the monster in the heart and frees the trapped animals. He then cut the monster into pieces, throwing them to the winds, creating the various Plateau tribes. However, one special tribe, the Nez Perce, were created from the blood on his hands, which he shook, sprinkling it throughout an area that then became traditional Nez Perce country.

The role of the Blue Jay in the religion and ceremonies of the Northwest Coast tribes is touched on in the Chinook myth (p. 141). It was no less important among several of the Plateau tribes, such as the Kalispel, Spokane, Coeur d'Alene, and Flathead, figuring prominently in their Winter Spirit Dance, one feature of which was the initiation of young men into communication with the higher powers, so enabling a guardian spirit to be found.

Raven, however, was perhaps one of the most important characters in several cultural areas. The mythology associated with the Blackfeet (Plains) Beaver Bundle, for example, refers to Raven as the wisest of all birds. His superior abilities were demonstrated in a tale referring to a contest with the Thunderbird, the Raven making it so cold that the only way Thunderbird could keep from freezing was by constantly flashing his lightning, finally conceding defeat.

For the Northwest Coast tribes, Raven was generally considered as the instrument of the creator. At the beginning of time he travelled around the world completing the task of creation and often became the benefactor to many tribes, bringing them food and gifts such as the Sun, Moon, and Stars. In the Kodiak Island (Arctic) myth (p. 129), Raven is credited with bringing light to the tribe, a recurring theme in several versions of this myth, the best known being that which refers to Raven stealing the Sun and hiding it in a box. He then traveled around the world opening the box – The Box of Daylight – thus giving light to the various sprits of the world as well as their physical forms. Some versions of this famous myth relate that prior to the liberation of light, Raven's feathers were white, the gradual release of the light turning them the colour of soot.

The Zuni (Southwest) legend of Spider Tower (p. 132), is a good example of how, in common with the other cultural areas, many features of the landscape – such as mountains, buttes, trails, and lakes – evoke mythological tales, which explain their formation or refer to them as sites of supernatural powers. Spider Tower is a well known site in the Canyon de Chelly and also figures in Navajo mythology, being the home of Spider Woman, who, obtaining inspiration from the spider web, was said to have taught the Navajo how to weave (see introduction to Chapter 2). Navajo myths also extend to explaining bizarre features of the rugged Southwestern landscape, such as the Black Rock or Cabezon Mountain. This strange geological feature, which is probably the eroded plug of a volcano, is said in Navajo mythology to be the head of a monster giant that was killed by the war gods (see Chapter 4). They cut off the monster's head, which then rolled down the mountain

PREVIOUS PAGE *Cherokee woman making pottery on the Qualla Reservation, North Carolina, photograph possibly by James Mooney, c. 1900. Excellent clay pottery – cups, pots and jugs – were made by the Southwestern Indians; they were either flat or round bottomed vessels depending on their use. A coiling technique was employed and the surfaces smoothed with a damp hide or cloth, as shown here.*

side to its present-day location, while the lava beds associated with the extinct volcano are described as its coagulated blood.

Two monsters, one male, one female, who kill hunters and children, are the subject of the Cherokee (Southeast) myth (p. 141). These monsters wore clothing made of stone and had sharp pointed hands, which were used to pierce the brains of the children that the female monster had captured. Such tales relating to creatures dressed in stone figure prominently in Cherokee mythology. One version has a stone man covered in a gigantic coat of small pieces of flint that he made after seeing a hunter kill a deer with a stone-pointed arrow. He caused havoc among the Cherokees, his favorite food being human livers; eventually he was captured, but before he died he relented and taught the Cherokees rituals, songs, and ceremonies that would help them in their quest for food and on the warpath.

The Cheyenne (Plains) tale of the Malicious Medicine Man (p. 135), draws attention to an important individual who figured in the majority of the cultural areas. Variously referred to as medicine men, priests, or shamans, their function was to achieve harmony between the tribe and the world of the spirits so that success in hunting, planting and the preventing of sickness and disease could be ensured. In this Cheyenne tale, however, the medicine man's power is misused and he is punished by a mystic buffalo bull.

Buffalo power, and also the importance of the eagle to the Plains Indian, are both touched on in this lengthy tale. In Plains society, both creatures were revered: the buffalo provided food, clothing, and shelter, indeed most of the Plains Indians' need for survival, and was viewed as a direct gift from Wakan-Tanka[8]. The greatly admired attributes of the eagle – its strength, courage, and beauty, together with its ability to soar above the clouds into the realm of the Great Sprit (manifested by the blue of the sky) – endowed it with mystical qualities. By the ritual use of its feathers on regalia and in ceremonies, it was considered possible to evoke the eagle spirit to act as a messenger between earth-bound man and the Gods and Goddesses.

The magpie, however, was held in much lesser esteem by the Sioux. Thus, in the legend of why the North Wind lost his birthright (p. 142; quoted from Walker, pp. 171-2) North Wind directs magpie to foul the tipi poles of a powerful wizard, who is so enraged that he causes the magpie's nest to be always fouled and the direction of the North Wind to be named after himself, Waziyata.

HOW LIGHT, FIRE, AND WATER ORIGINATED
(*Chippewa*)

Along time ago the only place where light could be seen was in the tipi of one old chief. This chief had light, fire, and water. All the other Indians in the whole world suffered from cold and darkness and had no water.

All the Indians came to this old chief's tipi and begged for a little light. He would not give them any. The Indians went away and told the wild animals, and asked their help.

The animals and the Indians held a great dance around the old chief's tipi. They chanted songs and all begged for light. Each one sang his own song.

One young fox kept singing, "Khaih! Khaih!" which means "Light." He believed it would bring light, and the men and the animals were helped, he was so strong. Their voices made a great noise.

At last a faint color was seen in the east. The old chief came out and drove the little light away.

Then the young fox called, "Khaih! Khaih!" louder than before. The men and the animals began again. They called and called for the light to come.

At last a little color was seen in the east again. The old chief had not slept. He was tired and he said: "You may have all the light you want."

Now the light comes every morning. Some of the animals still call for it to come before it is day.

A young caribou said that he would get the fire from the old chief's tipi. The Indians tied a great dry branch to his big antlers. The young caribou put his head in to the fire tipi and tried to reach the coals, but he could not do it. The wise chief drove him away.

Gab-gos-sha-de-bay, a Chippewa of the Mille Lac Band called by whites, Joe Broad, a grandson of Me-sig-un, a former chief, photographed by D. L. Gill in 1908. The man wears a headband with immature (white with brown or black tips) golden eagle feathers, a style typical of early Woodland headdresses. Across his left shoulder, is a magnificent bandolier bag with beaded floral designs.

Life in a Chippewa camp, photographed prior to 1929. Here, a woman is drying fish on the rack over a fire. Fish was an important part of the Chippewa diet; large fish were cut into strips and dried until hard and then packed into layers without salt. When needed for food, they were boiled.

Ne-gon-e-bin-ais or the Chippewa chief, 'Flat Mouth', laid out for burial. Photograph taken by Frances Densmore at Leech Lake, Minnesota, 24 July 1907. Parts of the ceremony of the Midewiwin Society are being conducted here. One after another, members of the Society sat beside the dead chief advising that he be careful on his journey to the spirit land.

But when the old chief was driving back the young caribou, muskrat crept into the tipi. He reached the precious coals and fire and caught one in his mouth. He ran back into the woods with it. Before he could reach his own burrow he had to drop the burning coal. It fell on the dry leaves and set the woods on fire. You can see now where the muskrat burned himself.

All the world had fire now, and there has always been enough since the muskrat dropped the first coal.

The fire melted the ice in the rivers and lakes. The light showed every one where to find water.

The old chief has never been seen since that time.

COYOTE KILLS THE GIANT
(*Flathead*)

Coyote came on up to Ravalli. There he met an Old Woman, who was camped close to where Ravalli Station is now. The Old Woman said to Coyote. "Where are you going?"

"Oh," said Coyote, "I am going to travel all over the world." "Well," said the Old woman, "you had better go back from here." "Why should I go back from here?" asked Coyote. "Because there is a Giant in this valley who kills every one that goes through," replied the Old Woman. "Well," said Coyote, "I will fight with him and kill him."

Then Coyote started on the trail again. He saw a great big tamarack-tree growing on the hillside, and he pulled it up and threw it over his shoulder and went on his way. He said to himself, "I'll choke that giant with this tamarack-tree. That's what I'll do."

Pretty soon he saw a woman that was nearly dead. "What is the matter with you?" asked Coyote, "Are you sick?"

The woman said, "No, I am not sick."

Coyote said, "I am going to choke the Giant with this tamarack-tree."

The woman said, "You might as well throw that stick away. Don't you know that you are already in the Giant's belly?"

Then Coyote threw the tamarack against the hillside, and it can be seen close to Arlee, a little station on the Northern Pacific Railroad. It stuck against the hillside and grew. All of what is now Jacko Valley was filled by the Giant's belly.

Angelic LaMoose, daughter of Joseph LaMoose, Indian scout on the Flathead Reservation. Photograph taken by H. T. Cory in September 1913. The beautiful heavy-fringed dress worn by this fine looking girl, the granddaughter of a chief, was made by herself and her mother; it is in a typical Plateau style with heavy cape and beaded and fringed skirt.

Selish-Delaware. 3.

Flathead Indians outside a canvas (?) tipi near Jocko, western Montana probably photographed about 1900. Although a Plateau tribe, the Flathead were greatly influenced by the Plains Indians to the east, from whom they obtained the idea of the tipi — their traditional dwellings, although conically shaped, were not portable. The tipi was generally used when travelling to the hunt (or powwow).

OPPOSITE *Tab-hetchet or 'Hand Shot Off', known to the whites as John Hill. Photographed by J. K. Hillers in January 1884. Tab-hetchet was 37 years old when this photograph was taken. Note the fine beaded and ermine skin fringed shirt which has definite Crow style characteristics.*

Coyote went on from there and he saw lots of people lying around. Some of them were dead, and some were pretty nearly dead. "What is the matter with you people?" asked Coyote.

They all said, "We are starving to death."

Coyote said, "What makes you starve? There is plenty to eat in here, lots of meat and fat."

Then Coyote cut chunks of grease from the sides of the Giant and fed them to the people, who got better. And then Coyote said, "Now, all of you people get ready to run out, I am going to cut the Giant's heart. When I start to cut you must all run out of O'Keef's Canyon or over at Ravalli."

The Giant's heart was the rounded cluster of mountains north of Flathead Agency, and there are marks on the side which show the place that Coyote cut with his stone knife.

Coyote began to cut the Giant's heart with his stone knife. Pretty soon the Giant said, "Please, Coyote, let me alone. You go out. I don't want you to stay in here. You can go out."

Coyote said, "No, I won't go out, I am going to stay right here. I'm going to kill you."

Then he started to cut the Giant's heart. He cut the Giant's heart off and then ran out. The Giant was dying, and his jaws began to close. Woodtick was the last to come out. The Giant's jaws were just closing down on him when Coyote caught him and pulled him out.

"Well," said Coyote, "you will always be flat. I can't help it now. You must be flat. That is the reason Woodtick is so flat.

127

Flathead family group, sometimes referred to as 'Interior Salish' to distinguish them from the Salishan tribes on the Northwest Coast. Photograph by James P. Christie, Montana, between 1890-1900. The girl wears a fine heavy leather belt, which appears to be decorated with beads and brass studs. The blanket worn by the man is a trade item possibly from the Pendleton Mills further north.

A group of St. Lawrence Island Eskimo children, photographed in 1888. St. Lawrence Island is part of the State of Alaska. The Eskimo who lived here were classed as Asiatic with basically the same culture as those on the nearby Siberian shore. Note the traditional hair-styles: the girl at the left has her hair long, while the tops of the boys' heads are shaved. Their clothing is of soft-tanned reindeer skin, hair-side in for warmth.

THE RAVEN
(Kodiak Island)

Light was not so universal formerly as now. Its cheering influences were then cast over one village only; and even there it depended on the caprices of the chief, who regulated and guarded it jealously. All other villages lived in darkness, although aware of the existence of light in that village. They made many attempts to get possession of it: some, after a few efforts, gave up in despair, others, not so easily discouraged, continued a longer time with the same empty result; and one village, owing to the persistent character of its chief, would never own itself defeated, and persevered in spite of past failures.

Here, in the village hall, the people gathered daily to discuss the all-important question of light, and concluded to call for volunteers to go in quest of it. To the fortunate one the following reward was held out – eternal glory, and the hand of the chief's beautiful and favorite daughter. Considering the inducements, there were no lack of volunteers at first, but, as none of these returned, not even to tell the story of the failure, the list became smaller and smaller, and after a time weeks would pass without any one offering himself. What became of these eager seekers after light was a mystery. It was generally supposed that some dropped by the wayside, and the others, on reaching the land of light, and finding the task too arduous, decided to remain there always rather than go back without light.

The chief, however, was undaunted, and continued calling the meetings and for volunteers regularly. At one of these the raven was present. He listened attentively to all the speeches, and heard the chief's call for volunteers, and when a considerable time had elapsed without any one indicating his desire to go, he

rose and addressed the assembly. Sad to say, his speech has been lost in the dark ages, except the last and memorable words: "I will bring you light." This was followed by such loud peals of laughter and mocking hoots that the building almost shook. The chief, who was deep in thought during the raven's harangue, was aroused from his revery by this sudden outburst of laughter, and inquired the cause of it. With much derision the speech and boasts of the raven were repeated to him. Although he may have had as little faith in the words of the raven as the others, he was yet too wise a man to let any opportunity, no matter how slim, of obtaining light – the great object of his life – go by unembraced. Instead of joining in the laughter, he mildly reproved his followers, and then addressing himself to the raven, congratulated him on his noble resolution, encouraged him to persevere, and ended by reminding him of the prize that awaited him whose efforts should be crowned with success.

With this the meeting dissolved. The raven, satisfied with the present and rejoicing in the future, flew home to make ready for the expedition. Joyfully he related the events of the day to his grandmother, a woman. "Caw! caw! caw! Grandmother, tomorrow I start after the light; and on my return with it I shall marry the chief's beautiful daughter and become famous. Make all things ready, for I leave early in the morning. Caw! caw! caw!"

"Ai-Ai-Yah!" she exclaimed. "Better ones than you have tried and failed, and how will you, a raven, get it? Why do you want to marry? Who will marry such a one as you? You smell too strong."

This was too much for him. "You old hag!" he screamed with rage. "Who is asking your opinion or advice? How does my smell concern you? You will not sleep with me. To spite you I will marry, and the chief's daughter at that. Even if I am a raven, I will do what I promise; and you do what I tell you, or you will be sorry."

Pacific Eskimo settlement, probably on Kodiak Island, photographed circa 1900. Their winter villages, as shown here, were generally located behind a headland or sheltered bay. Habitations were semi-subterranean dwellings covered with straw and turf (right) and could accommodate several families. The structure at the left was used for storage – above ground to protect the contents from animals.

She was sorry there and then, for he went at her with claws and bill till she begged for mercy, and promised to be more considerate in the future.

Early the next morning he left the village, and after several days of flight in the darkness it lightened up faintly. The farther he went, the lighter it became; and when he reached the village, the light was so strong that it almost blinded him. It was a large and cheerful village; the chief's large barrabara where the lights were kept, was in the center. Close by was a spring of water, and there the raven alighted and eyed sharply the women as they came for water. Not noticing the chief's daughter among them, he began to wish that she would appear. A moment later he saw her coming towards him; and when she had dipped out some water, he murmured, "I wish she would drink some of it." The words had barely been said when she bent over to drink. Instantly he changed himself into a tiny piece of down, and, unnoticed, she gulped it down with the water.

She conceived, and in due time gave birth to a son, a raven. Being the first child of an only child, he was fondled and nursed tenderly. The chief was especially devoted to him, and loved him even more than his daughter. He was indulged and humored in all his wishes. Whatever he saw he called for; whatever he called for had to be given to him; and if it was not given him immediately, he cawed, cried, pestered, clawed, and pecked until he got it. In this manner he handled everything on the premises that might possibly contain the lights, except three little caskets on an out of the way shelf. These he noticed one day, and asked for them. The chief was asleep, and as no one else dared touch them, the request was denied. But he would have them, and he commenced such a cawing, scratching, and hawing that the chief awoke. Not waiting to learn the cause of all this disturbance, he shouted angrily, "O, give him anything he wants and shut him up!" and went to sleep again.

The caskets were handed him, and he opened them one by one. In the first was night; the second contained the moon and stars; and in the third the sun was shining. He looked at them awhile, and then thrust them aside as worthless. But a few days later, when no one was about, he flew upon the shelf, grasped the two boxes containing the precious lights, and flew out with them. Some of the people outside noticed him, and raised the cry: "A raven flew out of the chief's barrabara with two boxes in his mouth!" When the chief discovered his loss, the raven was miles away.

He flew many days; and each day it grew darker and darker until he was in darkness altogether. After suffering some hardships he arrived in the village, reported himself to the chief, and requested that the people be called together. When all were assembled, he addressed them, congratulated them, reminded them of the last meeting, the promises made, and concluded by saying: "I have brought you light." In the presence of all he opened one of the caskets and instantly the moon and stars were visible in the sky. The people and chief were almost wild with joy; and the latter kept his promise, and bestowed on him his favorite daughter.

On the morrow the raven called on his father-in-law, and asked what he had to offer for a still better light than even the moon and stars, "My other daughter," replied the chief. "Call the people, and you shall have it," said the raven. If the villagers were wild with joy on seeing the moon and stars, imagine their emotions on beholding for the first time the sun. Since that memorable day the sun, moon and stars have illuminated the whole world. The crow married the two daughters of the chief, with whom he is living very happily to this day.

LEGEND OF SPIDER TOWER
(*Zuni*)

In Dead Man's Canyon – a deep gorge that is lateral to the once populated valley of the Rio de Chelly, Arizona – stands a stark spire of weathered sandstone, its top rising eight hundred feet above its base in a sheer uplift. Centuries ago an inhabitant of one of the cave villages was surprised by hostiles while hunting

LEFT *A Zuni woman weaving a belt, photographed by Christian Barthelmess, who was stationed at Fort Wingate and Fort Bayard, New Mexico, 1882-7. Women generally sat on the ground in front of their work and used little balls of yarn tied to the warp or to a simple bobbin for a shuttle. It was probably the Spanish who taught the use of hand looms, and the Zuni even adopted the western European band heddle.*

ABOVE *South front of the Zuni Pueblo in New Mexico, photograph by J. K. Hillers in 1879. The Pueblos consisted of large, often massive, structures, sometimes of stone but generally of adobe – large sun-dried bricks made of clay and straw – as shown here. Ladders allowed easy access to the several levels. Note the beehive-shaped ovens at the left.*

in this region, and was chased by them into this canyon. As he ran he looked vainly from side to side in the hope of securing a hiding-place, but succor came from a source that was least expected, for on approaching this enormous obelisk, with strength well-nigh exhausted, he saw a silken cord hanging from a notch at its top. Hastily knotting the end about his waist, that it might not fall within reach of his pursuers, he climbed up, setting his feet into roughnesses of the stone, and advancing, hand over hand, until he had reached the summit, where he stayed, drinking dew and feeding on eagles' eggs, until his enemies went away, for they could not reach him with their arrows, defended as he was by points of rock. The foemen having gone, he safely descended by the cord and reached his home. This help had come from a friendly spider who saw his plight from her perch at the top of the spire, and, weaving a web of extra thickness, she made one end fast to a jag of rock while the other fell within his grasp – for she, like all other of the brute tribe, liked the gentle cave-dwellers better than the remorseless hunters. Hence the name of the Spider Tower.

A Cheyenne parfleche exhibiting a design that dates back to at least the first half of the nineteenth century. These containers were made of rawhide; they were cut to shape rather like a giant envelope and then folded and painted. They were used to hold food or clothing.

MALICIOUS MEDICINE MAN
(*Cheyenne*)

Group of Southern Cheyennes taken by D. L. Gill during a delegation to Washington in 1909. At the back, left to right, are: Harvey Whiteshield, Joe Hamilton, and Robert H. Burns. Sitting, left to right, are Wolf Robe, Little Hand, Yellow Bear, White Eagle, and Mower. The Cheyenne people have been described as proud and brave, characteristics that show in the bold demeanour of the men here.

There was a great medicine-man, who was powerful and did injury, but who had a good daughter. He lived near a geyser, in an earth-lodge. Several young men lived with him, and went out hunting for him. He had great quantities of dried buffalo meat hanging all around his lodge. When meat was scarce in a village near by, he sent his young men to summon the people to him, and then he gave a feast to the various companies. Then this great man told the companies to dress, and dance before him. When the dance was almost over, he announced that he would pick out a young man to be his son-in-law. So he selected a young man, but after the marriage he sent the village away again. He was malicious, and did not treat his son-in-law rightly. Every night he had a fire, and slept close by his son-in-law and daughter. When they moved, he raised his head, and said: "Don't stir! Sleep!" When they talked, or even whispered, he made them be quiet, and ordered them to sleep. Even when they were outside, and spoke against him, he was so powerful that he knew it. The first morning he sent his son-in-law out to cut arrows. He told him that if he brought not smooth, straight sticks, he need not come back. The young man wandered through the woods, but he found only rough sticks, and he was discouraged, and tired, and cried. A person called him, and asked him why he wept. The young man related his trouble, and the person told him to cut bulrushes of the right length. So he got as many bulrushes as he could carry, and they turned to smooth sticks. Then he went on up a mountain, and cried again. The birds heard him, and asked him why he cried. He said that he could not get the eagle-feathers that his father-in-law wanted for feathering arrows. So the eagle shook himself, and feathers flew out, and he got as many as he could use. Then he returned, carrying the sticks and feathers. His father-in-law had four men who could make bows and arrows, and they began to make the arrows for him. Then he sent his son-in-law to get plums for the arrow-makers. It was nearly winter, and there was no fruit of any sort left, but he told him to get fresh plums, and bring none that were rotten or dried. He knew this was impossible. The young man took a bag, and went out, crying. Again a person asked him why he wept. The young man said it was because he was to get plums for the arrow-makers of his father-in-law. The person told him to go to a plum-bush and that the tree would shake itself, and only fresh plums would fall from it. All this happened. When the great medicine-man saw his son-in-law returning well loaded, he was pleased and went to meet him. So they made the arrows, and ate the plums. The next morning the great man wanted to play at throwing arrows at a hoop with his son-in-law. They played near the geyser, and the medicine-man pushed his son-in-law into it. Only his bones came out again.

Three times the great man had selected a son-in-law, and all this had happened. His daughter did not like his acts; but even when she went far off to tell her husband of his danger, the great man could hear by the wind or the earth what she said. The fourth time he got a very fine young man for son-in-law. He sent him out to drive a buffalo of good age immediately in front of his house, so that he could shoot him with his new arrows. The son-in-law went far off, crying. Seven buffalo were about him, and one asked him what he wanted. The young man told him, but they said they were powerless against this great man, and told him to go farther south. He went on, and met four buffalo, who asked him what he wished. But they also were powerless, and sent him farther south. He went on and came to two buffalo. With them the same happened. As he again went on southward, he was so discouraged that he walked with his head down, and when he met a single buffalo, did not stop even when the bull asked him what he wished. Finally he turned around, and told his story. He was hopeless, for the great man could not be cut or burnt or wounded in any way. "He is like this rock", he said, and pointed to a large black stone. Then the buffalo said: "I will try on this whether I can do anything to him." He went off east, and charged against the stone, but did not injure it. He charged from the south, from the west, from the north – all vainly. The fifth time he went toward the northeast, and this time be broke a piece out of the rock. Then he told the young man to drive him toward his father-in-law's house. They arrived there, both seeming completely tired out; the buffalo pretended to be trying to escape, while the young man headed him off. At last, after a long chase, he drove him near his father-in-law's door. The

OPPOSITE *Miovasu, a Southern Cheyenne woman and daughter of Cross Feathers. Photograph taken by D. L. Gill in 1908. This girl was only fifteen years old at the time the photograph was taken. She wears a magnificent cloth dress, the cape of which is decorated with elk teeth. The Cheyenne traditionally expected exceptionally high standards of women, and although polygamy was practiced, infidelity was abhorred.*

RIGHT *The Sun Dance Torture. Cheyenne warrior dragging buffalo skulls from thongs attached to his back. This photograph was taken a few miles east of Eagle City on the north fork of the Washita River. The Sun Dance ceremony was practiced in various forms by most Plains tribes. It evoked many mythological beings and powers of the Plains Indian cosmology.*

FOLLOWING PAGES *A cabin home on the Cherokee Qualla reservation in Swain and Jackson counties, North Carolina. Photograph taken by James Mooney in 1888. This cabin belongs to Ayyuini or 'Swimmer' who stands behind the woman (see also portrait photo, p. 140).*

medicine-man came out with his new arrows, and shot at the bull. When the arrows neared the buffalo, they turned to reeds again, and did not injure him; but to the medicine-man they appeared to enter the bull, and disappear in him. The bull staggered and seemed to nearly die, and the man approached him. The bull staggered farther and farther away from the house, leading the medicine-man with him, so that he might not escape. Then he turned, charged, and tossed him. As the man fell, he tossed him again and again, so that he never touched the ground. Thus he tossed him until he was completely bruised and unable to move. Then they put him in his lodge, and covered him with brush and wood and lit it. The flames burnt higher and higher, but they only heard the medicine-man inside the fire cursing and threatening them with death when he should come out. Then suddenly there were poppings, and explosions, and beads, diamonds, and precious stones flew out of the fire. They were afraid to touch these, for fear the man might then come to life again, and put them back into the fire. But the whites to whom some of them flew kept them, and thus became richer.

THE STONE-SHIELDS
(*Cherokee*)

In ancient times there lived among the Cherokees two strange beings – monsters of human form, resembling Cherokees in appearance. These two monsters, a man and a woman, lived in a cave. They were called Nayunu'wi (Stone-shields, or Stone-jackets), or Uilata (sharp, pointed), because they had sharp-pointed hands.

These monsters killed children, and sometimes adults. As they dressed like Cherokees, and spoke their language, it was difficult to distinguish them from this people.

The man generally killed hunters and other people who were alone and far from home, by attacking them. The woman used tricks to procure her victims. She came to the houses, kindly offering her services, offering to nurse children, and do similar things.

As soon as she had a child in her arms, she ran away with it, until she was out of hearing, and pierced the brain of the child with her hand, then took the liver from the body and disappeared. The Nayunu'wi appear to have lived on the livers of their victims.

The older Cherokees, long tired of the ravages of these monsters, held a council to determine the best way of killing the Uilata. At last they resolved to kill them with arrows, not knowing that the Uilata were stone clad. As soon as they saw an opportunity to attack the woman, they shot their arrows at her with all their might, but they were very much astonished to see that the arrows did not take the slightest effect.

Then a topknot-bird, which was perched on the branch of a tree close by, said to the warriors: "In the heart, in the heart."

The Cherokees shot their arrows at the spot where they supposed the heart to be, but no better than before did they succeed in killing the monster.

At last a jay appeared, and said to the warriors: "In the hand, in the hand!"

They shot the monster's hand, and it dropped dead. At the moment it fell its stone jacket broke into pieces. The people gathered the fragments, and kept them as sacred amulets, for luck in war, in hunting, and in love.

The man-monster disappeared; according to tradition, it went north.

The Cherokees possess also a legend about flying monsters having the form of falcons. These caught and killed especially children. They were slain by a brave man, whose little and only son had been captured by them. He followed them to their cave, where they kept their young, and killed the latter. Thereafter the old falcons disappeared forever.

BLUE JAY
(*Chinook*)

A mischievous deity of the Chinooks and other western peoples is Blue Jay. He is a turbulent braggart, schemer, and mischief-maker. He is the very clown of gods, and invariably in trouble himself if he is not manufacturing it for others. He has the shape of a jay-bird, which was given him by the Supernatural People because he lost to them in an archery contest. They placed a curse upon him, telling him the note he used as a bird would gain an unenviable notoriety as a bad omen. Blue Jay has an elder brother, the Robin, who is continually upbraiding him for his mischievous conduct using sententious phrases. The story of the many tricks and pranks played by Blue Jay, not only on the long-suffering members of his tribe, but also upon the denizens of the supernatural world, must have afforded intense amusement around many an Indian camp-fire. Even the proverbial gravity of the Red Man could scarcely hold out against the comical adventures of this American Owlglass.

HOW THE NORTH WIND LOST HIS BIRTHRIGHT
(*Sioux*)

The directions moved from place to place over the world so the Wind told the Four Winds to mark the directions so that each of them would know where he belonged. He told them that the North Wind, as the oldest, ought to have the first direction, which must be farthest from the Sun. He told them to put a great pile of stones at each direction so that it would be forever marked. When they were going to the edge of the world to mark the directions, the wizard met them. Because the North Wind was surly and a coward the wizard took from him the birthright of the oldest and gave it to the West wind. Then he made it cloudy so that the Sun could not be seen, and guided them to the edge of the world. A little bird told them to set up a pile of stones there. They did so. When the Sun was leaving the world he passed very near to them. Then they knew that that was the direction of the West Wind and that it would always be considered the first. Then the Four Winds traveled together until they came to the place where the Sun was furthest from them. There they saw the tipi of the wizard and he invited them inside. They all went inside except the North Wind who said that his tipi should be where the tipi of the wizard stood and that he was afraid of the wizard. Then he told a magpie to sit on the poles of the tipi and befoul the wizard when he came through the door. When the magpie did this the wizard said that because of this it should befoul its nest forever. So to this time magpies befoul their nests. Then he told the North Wind that because he had made the magpie do a nasty thing, the wind should be the wizard's messenger forever and that he, the wizard, would take the first place in the name of the direction of the North Wind. This is why the direction of the North Wind is called Waziyata.

A Dakota woman cooking in front of a tipi with corn and strips of meat drying on racks. Photograph by D. F. Barry. These appear to be canvas tipis, material that was government issue from the 1880s. The buffalo had been virtually exterminated; nevertheless several large hides, possibly buffalo, are staked out on the ground illustrating the common method of tanning.

Umbilical cord container, probably Sioux. After birth, the cord was preserved generally in an attractively beaded container, as shown here. It was attached to the cradle and later to the belt of the youngster. The lizard-like shape evokes the power of survival associated with this creature and tended to be associated with male children. Turtle-shapes were associated with females, a sign of fertility.

A Lakota warrior on horseback, a figure in beadwork on a pipe-bag. This is typical Teton Sioux (Lakota) beadwork for the period, last quarter of the nineteenth century. Note the fine details of the eagle feather headdress, the tied tail for battle, and the scalp hanging from the horse's bridle.

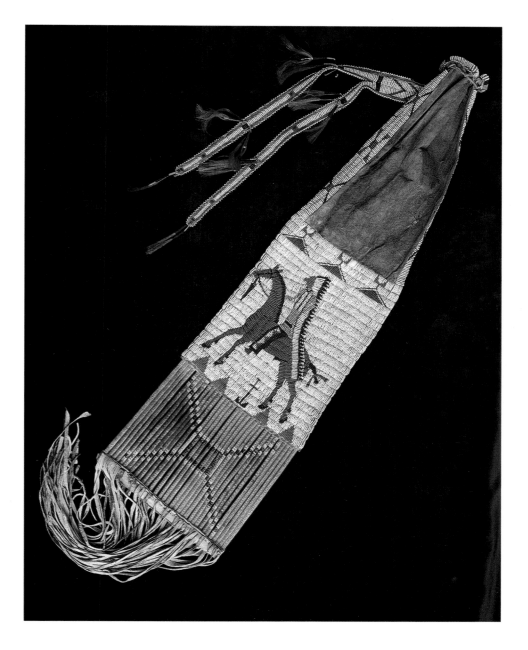

Mythology and Lore of Tribal Customs

ANY MYTHS, particularly the more complex, led to a fundamental pattern of living, in some ways regimenting the population, and various components of ceremonies and rituals were often described as having been given to humans in ancient times by the spirit. Many ceremonies were a dramatization of the origin or other sacred myths, which were said to refer to ancestral or human events. The myths, particularly those referring to origins, tended to establish the nature of interaction between humans and the natural and supernatural worlds, serving not only as a medium of instruction, but also establishing codes of conduct; those who neglected the various obligations dictated by the ceremonies, ran the risk of offending the spirits.

The Midwinter Festival of the Iroquois contains one episode that involves the powerful False Face Society, the members of which, when they donned masks of fantastical designs, were credited with special abilities. In myths relating to the formation of the Society, a giant was said to have opposed the Creator, and in a contest of strength that involved the moving of a mountain, the Creator shifted it close by with surprising ease, whereupon – in an unguarded moment – the giant smashed his nose against its peak. The masks worn by some members of the False Face Society refer to this mythological episode, the nose being carved in a twisted shape – hence, Old Broken Nose. The legend continues to explain that, conceding defeat, the giant promises the Creator that he will act as a healer, and this becomes an important function in the activities of the False Face Society.

Events that occurred after the formation of the world by the Creator, are the subject of the Onondaga False Face myth (p. 148). Here, another version of the moving mountain episode is related and the giant is now already ugly, his face being red and twisted with the mouth pulled up at one corner. However, the agreement struck between the Creator and the giant to cure people and the associated dances in the False Face Longhouse form the main body of the narrative.

The importance of the buffalo to the Plains tribes is illustrated by the Cheyenne and Pawnee myths (p. 148 and 154). In particular, the Pawnee myth draws attention to the widespread buffalo-calling ceremonies, which were a marked feature of both the Plains and Southwestern cultures. The references to the buffalo herds emerging from a mountain in the Cheyenne myth is common to myths of other Plains Algonquian, such as the Arapaho, Blackfeet, and Cree. Thus in the complex and ancient Beaver Bundle ceremony of the Blackfeet, one important duty of the Beaver Men was to take on the role of buffalo-callers. Part of the ceremony consisted of a series of songs in groups of four or seven, where reference is made to the buffalo in the mountains, such as:

> The Buffalo likes to live in the mountains during the autumn.
> He comes down from the mountains to the plains
> The mountains are his medicine'
>
> (Piegan Beaver Medicine Song. McClintock, p. 82)

Buffalo-calling was also an important episode in the complex O-kee-pa ceremony of the Mandan, where the fate of those who attempt to disrupt the ceremonies is illustrated by the antics of the mythological Foolish One (p. 152; quoted from Bowers, p. 365) or, as he is also referred to, the Evil Spirit, O-ke-hee-de. This trickster-type character attempts to disrupt the buffalo dances by darting among the spectators and then making towards the dancers. He wore an artificial penis, 'of colossal dimensions, pendulous as he ran and extending somewhat below his knees' (Catlin, 1967, p. 83). This, he erected as he approached the women and dancers, but was suddenly and dramatically held in check by the medicine pipe carried by the leader of the ceremonies. His power now dissipated, he was set upon by the women who tore off his accoutrements and regalia and drove him out on to the prairie.

The Medicine Bundle complex so common to Plains Indian culture is referred to in the Pawnee myth of the Sacred Bundle (p. 166). The mythological origin of medicine bundles as a gift from the supreme deity, Ti-ra-wa (abbreviated from Tirawahat), is referred to here. The most important bundles among the Pawnee were generally considered to be tribally owned and, as with several other Plains tribes,

PREVIOUS PAGE *The white Deerskin Dance of the Hupa Indians, who occupied northwestern California. Photograph by A. W. Erikson, circa 1890-1900. This is one of the three main annual dances of the Hupa and was both a world renewal and wealth display ceremony. Participants, as shown here, held albino or other unusual deerskins aloft on poles and carried large obsidian blades wrapped around with a piece of buckskin. An Athapaskan tribe, the Hupa were almost unique among the Californian Indians in their preoccupation with wealth and status.*

they contained a variety of objects that were considered sacred because of their powers as pronounced by the sacred beings. Pawnee religion put great emphasis on Sky Powers, their Star Bundles, for example, were said to have been made up according to instructions received from the Morning and Evening Stars and other celestial bodies. These not infrequently contained fragments of meteorites, which were said to be messengers from the Sky Powers; they were opened at the first thunder of spring, being used in ceremonies that gave thanks to the higher powers for the continued cycle of life on earth.

The Lakota (Teton Sioux) Sun Dance was called Wiwanyangwacipi, literally 'Sun-looking-as-they-dance', and its mythological origins are described in the chapter (p. 160; quoted from Walker, pp. 212-15). In the myths of the North American Indians, as in the mythology of many peoples, the sun figured prominently. Thus, among the Natchez (Southeastern cultural area), there was a belief that the universe was filled with spirits in human forms but that there were differences in power among them. However, 'the most powerful of all [was] a sky deity resident in or connected with the Sun' (Swanton, 1911, p. 174). Many other tribes held a similar belief, although there were considerable variations in interpretation. For example, the Lakota Red Bird explained that his people perceived 'a mysterious power greater than all others, which is represented by nature, one form of representation being the sun. [So] we made sacrifices to the sun, and our petitions were granted' (Densmore, p. 86).

In the latter half of the nineteenth century the Sun Dance was performed in various forms by most Plains tribes, generally taking place in the summer and lasting up to eight days. In whatever form, however, it was always perceived as a gruelling and testing ordeal for the main participants – although the complex ceremony, which involved the gathering of a scattered tribe, obviously acted as an important seasonal unifying factor. In the Lakota Sun Dance, it was considered that the penitent offered to Wakan-Tanka, approximately translated to 'Great Spirit', that which was strongest in his training and nature – the ability to endure physical pain. This was done as a fulfilment of a vow made in time of great anxiety, such as on the warpath or during illness, in order to secure health and prosperity. One extreme component of the ritual – undertaken by only the most dedicated – was the piercing of the muscles of the chest or back by skewers of wood or bone. These were tied by long thongs to the central Sun Dance circle pole and the penitent then danced to pull them free.

THE FALSE FACES
(*Onondaga*)

After he had made the world and its people, Rawen Niyoh left it for a time, but when he returned he was one day walking through an open place, following the sun, overlooking his own work, and examining the ground where the people were going to live, when his eye caught a strange, long-haired figure coming in the opposite direction. The face of this figure was red and twisted, the mouth being pulled up at the left corner.

Rawen Niyoh said to him, "Where did you come from?" to which the False Face replied, "I am the real owner of this world - I was here before you."

Rawen Niyoh said, "I think I am the owner of this place, because I made it."

"That may be quite true," the False Face assented, "but I have been here a long time, and I have a good claim to it, and I am stronger than you are."

"Show me how you can prove this," demanded Rawen Niyoh.

The False Face suggested that they should retire to a valley not far from two high mountains. The False Face ordered one of the mountains to come nearer, and it moved close to them. Rawen Niyoh was very much surprised at the result, upon which he ordered the other mountain to approach, which it did - the two remaining so nearly together that Rawen and the False Face had barely room to get out.

Each was satisfied with this exhibition of power on the part of the other, and Rawen Niyoh said, "I think it would not be well for you to be seen here by the people who are coming to this place, because you are so ugly, for everybody would follow you to look at you."

Ah k'on wa-rah (the False Face) agreed to this on condition that he should be allowed to claim the new people as his grandchildren and they were to call him Grandfather. "I will help all I can," said he "to drive away sickness from among the new people, and I am able to protect them from storms by causing the winds to go up high into the sky."

Rawen Niyoh replied, "I am sure you have much power to help the people, and you must keep this power as long as they live. We will make a bargain. They shall be your grandchildren, and you their Grandfather. They must observe a dance – the False Face Dance – at the Longhouse, forever. Now we make this bargain, which shall last as long as you, and I, and the people, and the world shall last."

Ah k'on wa-rah replied, "It is well, and I want you to know that I am going to get much help in my good work among the people, from my brother who is black, and who will be with me, as well as from my cousin who always goes with us. He is half black and half red."

Rawen Niyoh and Ah k'on wa-rah then separated, the former saying, "I am going towards the setting sun," and the Red False Face saying "I go where the sun rises."

It will be seen from this story that even Rawen Niyoh is not supreme. His power is equalled by that of Ah k'on-wa-rah, and both are able to transport themselves to any part of the world at pleasure.

THE BUFFALO KEEPERS
(*Cheyenne*)

Far away there was a large camp-circle. Food was very scarce, and some persons had starved. One day one of the old men went about inquiring whether the people wanted to travel to a large lake, where ducks and game abounded. They moved camp, packing their goods on dogs. Two young men were sent ahead, but they returned with the news that they had found no game whatever. The children were all crying for food, and the misery was extreme. The people selected two strong young men able to travel for four days without food, and told them that they must find something for the whole tribe, and bring back good news.

Buffalo dancers of the Cheyenne. Photograph possibly by Edward S. Curtis, prior to 1927. These two women are wearing buffalo headdresses, which consisted of the scalp and part of the mane with the horns attached. The buffalo was a highly revered animal, it represented long life and plenty and many ceremonies were held in its honor and, not least, myths were recounted in its creation.

The young men set out and traveled steadily for two days, until they were worn out and slept from the middle of the night until the morning star rose. Then they went on northward again. Finally they came near a large river, and beyond it they saw a blue mountain.

The river was slow, smooth, wide, and sandy on both sides, but beyond it rose bluffs, and close behind these the mountain. The two scouts put their clothes on their heads, and entered the river. In the center, one of them was held fast. He shouted that some powerful thing under water was taking him; and he asked his friend to tell his parents not to weep too much for him. The other man crossed in safety. Then his friend called to him to come back and touch him as a farewell. So the other went back into the river, and touched him. Then he went out again, and cried all day, wandering about. A person came to the top of the bank above the river, and asked him why he cried, and whether he could do anything for him. The young man replied that a powerful animal was holding fast his friend in the river, and pointed to him. The person who had come was powerful; he wore a wolfskin, painted red, on his back; it was tied around his neck and wrist, so that he looked like a wolf, and he carried a large knife. He dived into the river, and the water moved and waved, and finally an immense snake with black horns came up and he cut its throat. The man who had been

The tipi of Issiwun, the Sacred Buffalo Hat of the Northern Cheyenne. Photograph by James Mooney about 1906. According to the historian of the Cheyenne, Father Peter Powell, the object hanging on a pole above the sacred tipi is Nimhoyah, 'The Turner', a red painted disc of rawhide, trimmed with buffalo tails. It was so-called because this sacred object could turn both death and sickness away from the Cheyenne camps. Issiwun was (and still is) a great symbol and source of female renewing power. Together with the Mahuts or 'Four Sacred Arrows', these are holy objects with associated rich tribal mythology.

held fast was already cold and stiff in his legs, but the two others dragged him off, and floated him ashore, and laid him in the sun. The rescuer told the other young man: "Go to the mountain, to its stone door, and tell your grandmother that I have killed the animal that I have been after so long." The young man ran to the foot of the mountain, stood before a flat stone door, and called as he had been told, telling the woman to bring rope with her. The old woman was glad that the animal had at last been killed. The young man ran back, and was told by the man to help him butcher the snake; then they would carry his friend to his house. They dragged the snake on shore by its horns, and cut it in two, and then into many smaller pieces. They made many trips to the mountain, carrying the meat.

Inside, the mountain was like the interior of a tipi, with tent-poles, beds, and so on. Then the young man carried his friend to the mountain, taking him on his back, and holding his hands. The woman made a sweat-house, and he was put into it. The woman told him to try to move. The second time they poured water on the hot rocks he moved a little, the third time more, and after the fourth time he was perfectly well. Then they went into the mountain, and the man told his daughter to cook food, corn and buffalo meat. This was the first time the young men had seen the daughter, who was very handsome. They ate all the food given them, and were well satisfied. Then the woman asked them why they had come. They told her that they were looking for game for their starving people. The woman said: "It is well, you will have something for your tribe." Then she asked them what kin they would be to the girl; whether they would be her brothers. While they conferred, she said that they could marry her. The other young man proposed to the one that had been held fast that he should marry her, and the latter agreed. They were then all very grateful to each other, and the young man married the girl. The woman told her daughter to take the two young men to the herd of buffalo, and the girl showed them large herds of buffalo, and on the other side wide fields of corn. Then the woman told them to cross the river in the same place as before, and not to look backwards, and to rest four times on their way home.

So they traveled for four days. Then an old man cried through the village that they were coming. All their relatives and many others came forward; but when they saw that there were three persons, they held somewhat aloof. They entered a tent, and the new husband told an old man to cry to the people to come to shake hands with his wife and embrace her. This was done, and then the young man said that he brought good news, and that that same night his wife's herd would come from the mountain. At night long strings of buffalo came and the people heard them on all sides. Early in the morning they saw the buffalo, as far as they could look. It was announced that the dogs were not to disturb the game. Then the hunt commenced. The buffalo ran when pursued, but always came back. As many were killed as could be used, and there was an abundance of meat. The chiefs gathered, and resolved that they were thankful to the girl for her kindness, and every family was to bring her a present, the best that they had; and they asked her to take the presents to her parents. So all gave to her, and she started back to her parents with her husband and his friend. When they arrived at the mountain, her father stood there, calling to his wife to come out, for their son-in-law had returned. She embraced the two young men from joy and gratitude. When they returned, the tribe was still hunting successfully, and they were again given presents to bring to the girl's parents.

When they brought presents a second time, the girl's father was still more grateful, and asked his daughter to take a few ears of corn to the tribe. But, she, thinking that they had enough with the buffalo, was silent. When her parents asked her why she did not answer, she told them the reason. So they returned, after her parents had warned her not to feel sorry for any buffalo killed in her sight. Soon after, the children drove a young calf toward the village, and the boys shot at it, and it died in front of her tent. As she came out, she said to herself that she pitied the calf. But as she said it, the herd ran back toward the mountain and nothing could be seen but dust. A crier went about, saying that presents must again be sent to the old man in the mountain. After prayer and with blessings, the two young men and the girl started once more. After four days they arrived. At once the old man told his daughter that she ought to have been careful. But he would not let them return to the tribe. The parents of the young men and their relatives felt lonely at the long absence, and went out alone to cry. But the young men never returned.

O-KEE-PA CEREMONY: THE FOOLISH ONE
(*Mandan*)

Once there was a woman in the village who had never been around with young men. While returning from her field with the other women she brushed into some burrs, and they fastened to her dress. She went into the lodge to take off the dress and remove the burrs. It was dark in the lodge, so she stood under the opening where the smoke went out. Suddenly she saw a shadow at the smokehole, and she hid herself. In a short time she heard someone inside her singing, and it nearly killed her. In the night a child was born to her, and it disappeared as soon as it was born. She called all the family, and they buildt a bright fire. The child was black. He kept jumping up and down, and they could not do anything with him.

He grew very fast and was never still. He was always running and jumping about. One day his grandfather was making up arrows and tipping them with wing feathers of the speckled eagle. The boy liked them and wanted them over his shoulder in a sheath. The boy took the arrows and went out. This was the first time he had ever been out of the earth lodge, for the people were afraid that he would run away. When he got outside the earth lodge, he ran about, making great leaps, running up the earth lodges, and flitting around to the entertainment of the people.

But this little black boy ran out onto the hills where he killed the sacred snakes and many other holy things. He even killed the wicked women who lived in the earth and crept out at dark to entice men away from their wives. He would not stay away from the sacred things. Finally, all the spirits of the sacred things got together and vowed that he must be killed.

ABOVE *A Mandan Medicine Lodge. The typical dwelling of the Mandans was a round earth-covered lodge, and such earth lodges were clustered around a central village plaza in which stood a cedar post surrounded by a small palisade. The post represented the kindly mythological figure, 'First Man', who was said to have made everything. The Medicine Lodge is identified by its flat front, inherited from a more archaic structure. The O-kee-pa ceremony was performed in the central plaza where 'Foolish One' performed his bizarre antics.*

One day there was a heavy fog sent by the spirits of the holy things. When it cleared up, Foolish One was not to be found. In a short time his father came looking for him. His father must have been the Sun or lived in the Sun. He found the boy dead and was very angry. All the people of the village had liked him even though he had been so foolish. The father was very angry and demanded of Lone Man who had killed his son. All the spirits that had helped kill little Foolish One became frightened of the Sun spirit and hid in a hole on the top of the Killdeer Mountains. At that time the mountains were solid. The spirit from the Sun hit the mountain with his club and broke it into two parts, so that today there are two parts, the head and the body.

Big Foolish One asked Lone Man what should be done with the little fellow. They came to a big rock, and Lone Man split it with his lance. They put the boy in the rock and fitted the rock back. This rock is near one of our camps on the Heart River. Big Foolish One went back to the Sun, and he never came back again. Many still worship him as a great spirit, and we put him in the O-kee-pa on one of the days of dancing because he was here on earth when Lone Man was here.

RIGHT Eagle Woman, a Mandan lady, sewing quill designs on buckskin. Her daughter was part Hidatsa, a closely related tribe at this time (circa 1900). Both Mandan and Hidatsa lived on the same reservation, Fort Berthold in North Dakota. The large disc that Eagle Woman is working on is probably for a blanket band; smaller areas, such as the bands on shirts and leggings were quicker and probably easier to produce.

LEFT *Petalesharro, photographed in 1871. According to Garland Blame (Hereditary Head Chief of the Pawnee in 1976), this man was Head Chief of all Pawnees and Villages and was of the Chaui band. The photographer, W. H. Jackson, stated that he was considered a good orator and was of dignified bearing. He wears a magnificent eagle feather horned bonnet and leggings and garters decorated with beadwork. Note the pipe tomahawk with the heart design in the blade that he carries in his left hand.*

THE MAN WHO CALLED THE BUFFALO
(*Pawnee*)

This happened in the olden time before we had met the white people. Then the different bands lived in separate villages. The lodges were made of dirt. The Kit-ka-hahk'-i band went off on a winter hunt, roaming over the country, as they used to do, after buffalo. At this time they did not find the buffalo nearby. They scouted in all directions, but could discover no signs of them. It was a hard time of starvation. The children cried and the women cried: they had nothing at all to eat.

There was a person who looked at the children crying for something to eat, and it touched his heart. They were very poor, and he felt sorry for them. He said to the head chief: "Tell the chiefs and other head men to do what I tell them. My heart is sick on account of the suffering of the people. It may be that I can help them. Let a new lodge be set up outside the village for us to meet in. I will see if I can do anything to relieve the tribe." The chief said that it was well to do this, and he gave orders for it.

While they were preparing to build this lodge they would miss this man in the night. He would disappear like a wind, and go off a long way, and just as daylight came he would be there again. Sometimes, while sitting in his own lodge during the day, he would reach behind him, and bring out a small piece of buffalo meat, fat and lean, and would give it to some one, saying, "When you have had enough, save what is left, and give it to some one else." When he would give this small piece of meat to any one, the person would think, "This is not enough to satisfy my hunger," but after eating until he was full, there was always enough left to give to some other person.

In those days it was the custom for the head chief of the tribe, once in a while, to mount his horse, and ride about through the village, talking to the people, and giving them good advice, and telling them that they ought to do what was right by each other. At this time the chief spoke to the people, and explained that this man was going to try to benefit the tribe. So the people made him many fine presents, otter skins and eagle feathers, and when they gave him these things each one said: "I give you this. It is for yourself. Try to help us." He thanked them for these presents, and when they were all gathered together he said: "Now you chiefs and head men of the tribe, and you people, you have done well to give me these things. I shall give them to that person who gives me that power, and who has taken pity on me. I shall let you starve yet four days. Then help will come."

View of a Pawnee Indian Village, photographed in Nebraska in 1871. Large crowds are seated on the earth lodge roofs probably to witness a ceremony that is taking place in the village plaza. Pawnee ceremonies were predominately concerned with heavenly bodies and cosmic forces.

ABOVE *A Pawnee earth lodge at Loup Fork Village, Nebraska. Photograph by W. H. Jackson in 1871. Such earth lodges generally housed several families. The Pawnee, as with most Missouri River tribes, were semi–sedentary and only used the tipi on certain occasions, such as hunting trips. Note the long tipi poles leaning against the entrance to the earth lodge.*

OPPOSITE *Wife of Coming Sun, Pawnee, probably taken at the World Fair, St Louis, Missouri in 1904. Coming Sun, or Saku:ru Ta, was best known as James Murie, whose mother was Skidi Pawnee and whose father was a white man. The Murie family had a deep interest in Pawnee cosmology and mythology, contributing immensely to the scientific literature. Mrs Murie is wearing a beautiful buckskin dress, the cape is heavily fringed and embellished with much-coveted elk teeth.*

During these four days, every day and night he disappeared, but would come back the same night. He would say to the people that he had been far off, where it would take a person three or four days to go, but he was always back the same night. When he got back on the fourth night, he told the people that the buffalo were near, that next morning they would be but a little way off. He went up on the hill near the camp, and sacrificed some eagle feathers, and some blue beads, and some Indian tobacco, and then returned to the camp. Then he said to the people, "When that object comes to that place of sacrifice, do not interfere with it; do not turn it back. Let it go by. Just watch and see."

The next morning at daylight, all the people came out of their lodges to watch this hill, and the place where he had sacrificed. While they were looking, they saw a great buffalo bull come up over the hill to the place. He stood there for a short time and looked about, and then he walked on down the hill, and went galloping off past the village. Then this man spoke to the people and said, "There. That is what I meant. That is the leader of the buffalo: where he went the whole herd will follow."

He sent his servant to the chiefs to tell them to choose four boys, and let them go to the top of the hill where the bull had come over, and to look beyond it. The boys were sent, and ran to the top of the hill, and when they looked over beyond it they stopped, and then turned and came back running. They went to the chiefs' lodge and said to the chiefs, sitting there, "Beyond that place of sacrifice there is coming a whole herd of buffalo; many, many, crowding and pushing each other."

Then, as it used to be in the old times, as soon as the young men had told the chief that the buffalo were coming, the chief rode about the village, and told everyone to get ready to chase them. He said to them besides: "Do not leave anything on the killing ground. Bring into the camp not only the meat and hides, but the heads and legs and all parts. Bring the best portions in first, and take them over to the new lodge, so that we may have a feast there." For so the man had directed.

Presently the buffalo came over the hill, and the people were ready, and they made a surround, and killed all that they could, and brought them home. Each man brought in his ribs and his young buffalo, and left them there at that lodge. The other parts they brought into the village, as he had directed. After they

had brought in this meat, they went to the lodge, and stayed there four days and four nights, and had a great feast, roasting these ribs. The man told them that they would make four surrounds like this, and to get all the meat that they could. "But," he said, "in surrounding these buffalo you must see that all the meat is saved. Ti-ra'wa does not like the people to waste the buffalo, and for that reason I advise you to make good use of all you kill." During the four nights they feasted, this man used to disappear each night.

On the night of the fourth day he said to the people: "Tomorrow the buffalo will come again, and you will make another surround. Be careful not to kill a yellow calf – a little one – that you will see with the herd, nor its mother." This was in winter, and yet the calf was the same color as a young calf born in the spring. They made the surround, and let the yellow calf and its mother go.

Kithkhabki or Republican Pawnee group, photographed by W. H. Jackson in 1868-9 or 1871. The men are identified, left to right as: 'Stopped with Horses'; 'Humane Chief'; 'As a Dog but yet a High Chief'; 'Good Chief' and 'Difficult Chief'. Note the leggings embellished with bear-paw images in beadwork worn by 'Humane Chief'; bear power was particularly important to most Plains tribes.

A good many men in the tribe saw that this man was great, and that he had done great things for the tribe, and they made him many presents, the best horses that they had. He thanked them, but he did not want to accept the presents. The tribe believed that he had done this wonderful thing, had brought them buffalo, and all the people wanted to do just what he told them to.

In the first two surrounds they killed many buffalo, and made much dried meat. All their sacks were full, and the dried meat was piled up out of doors. After the second surround, they feasted as before.

After four days, as they were going out to surround the buffalo the third time, the wind changed, and, before the people could get near them, the buffalo smelled them and stampeded. While they were galloping away, the man ran up on the top of the hill, to place a sacrifice, carrying a pole, on which was tied the skin of a kit fox; and when he saw the buffalo running, and that the people could not catch them, he waved his pole, and called out Ska-a-a-a! and the buffalo turned right about, and charged back right through the people, and they killed many of them. He wished to show the people that he had the power over the buffalo.

After the third surround they had a great deal of meat, and he called the chiefs together and said, "Now, my chiefs, are you satisfied?" They said, "Yes, we are satisfied, and we are thankful to you for taking pity on us and helping us. It is through your power that the tribe has been saved from starving to death." He said: "You are to make one more surround, and that will be the end. I want you to get all you can. Kill as many as possible, for this will be the last of the buffalo this winter. Those presents that you have made to me, and that I did not wish to take, I give them back to you." Some of the people would not take back the presents, but insisted that he should keep them, and at last he said he would do so.

The fourth surround was made, and the people killed many buffalo and saved the meat. The night after this last surround he disappeared and drove the buffalo back. The next morning he told the people to look about, and tell him if they saw anything. They did so, but they could not see any buffalo.

The next day they moved camp, and went east toward their home. They had so much dried meat that they could not take it all at once, but had to come back and make two trips for it. When they moved below, going east, they saw no fresh meat, only dried meat; but sometimes when this man would come in from his journeys, he would bring a piece of meat, a little piece, and he would divide it up among the people, and they would put it into the kettles and boil it, and everybody would eat, but they could not eat it all up. There would always be some left over. This man was so wonderful that he could change even the buffalo chips that you see on the prairie into meat. He would cover them up with his robe, and when he would take it off again, you would see there pounded buffalo meat and tallow (pemmican), tup-o-har'us.

The man was not married; he was a young man, and by this time the people thought that he was one of the greatest men in the tribe, and they wanted him to marry. They went to one of the chiefs, and told him that they wanted him to be this man's father-in-law, for they wanted him to raise children, thinking that they might do something to benefit the tribe. They did not want the race to die out. The old people say that it would have been good if he had had children, but he had none. If he had, perhaps they would have had the same power as their father.

That person called the buffalo twice, and twice saved the tribe from a famine. The second time the suffering was great, and they held a council to ask him to help the tribe. They filled up the pipe, and held it out to him, asking him to take pity on the tribe. He took the pipe, and lighted it and smoked. He did it in the same way as the first time, and they made four surrounds, and got much meat.

When this man died, all the people mourned for him a long time. The chief would ride around the village and call out: "Now I am poor in mind on account of the death of this man, because he took pity on us and saved the tribe. Now he is gone and there is no one left like him."

This is a true and sacred story that belongs to the Kit-ka-hahk-'i band. It happened once long ago, and has been handed down from father to son in this band.

LAKOTA SUN DANCE
(*Sioux*)

In their winter camp the Lakota were hungry and the little children cried for meat. In a visitation a shaman was told that if a man would go west he would be taught how the people could get food. At the council a young man offered to go, so the people gave him a pouch with a little food in it. He went westward and saw an old woman. She asked him for food and he gave her his pouch. She ate ravenously and he thought she would eat all his food, but he sang a song of joy and looked westward while she ate. She watched him and when she had finished eating she returned the pouch to him and told him that she was Wakanka, the Old Woman, and because he had cheerfully given her all his food he should never be hungry. He looked at the pouch and it was full of good food. Ever after it remained full, no matter how often or how much he took from it. The old woman said that the weather was cold and the snow deep, and no one would travel except from necessity.

She then gave him a robe made of woven rabbit skins, very light and very warm, and moccasins lined with otter fur, the soles of which were thick and springy like a bow. She told him to go to a hill in the west and there someone would tell him where to go. He went as she told him. The robe was so light that it kept him from sinking in the snow and the soles of his moccasins were so springy that they shot him forward like an arrow. Soon he came to a hill and saw an old man sitting on it. The old man said he was very cold for he had no robe. The young man gave him the rabbit-skin robe. The old man said, "I am Wazi, the Wizard. Because you have given me your robe you shall never be cold." He told him to go to a cave and someone there would guide him, but if he should see a young man not to listen to him.

Lakota dancing and celebrating the 50th Anniversary of the founding of the Rosebud Agency in South Dakota, 1929. This shows much traditional costume of the Plains Sioux from circa 1890 onwards. Note the fine hair pipe breast plate, together with the hair roach worn by the figure in the foreground (center); another (to his right) wears an eagle feather war bonnet, others wear otter fur collars and dance bells.

Lakota Sun Dance at the 50th Anniversary Celebrations of the founding of the Rosebud Agency. Photograph by Bert Bell from 1929. This man is blowing on the eagle wing bone whistle to which are attached feathers and buckskin (probably quilled) thongs. He is looking towards the central Sun Dance pole, with his right hand raised to honor its power.

The young man went westward; the weather was warm and there was no snow. He saw another young man going westward and soon overtook him. This young man asked him where he was going and why he traveled so fast. The young man did not answer and continued to travel. The stranger traveled with him and as fast as he did, asking many questions, but the young man would not speak. Then the stranger said he could tell how the young man could travel still faster. When the young man asked how that could be done, he said that his two moccasin soles made him travel fast, but that if he had four moccasin soles he would travel twice as fast. The young man asked how he could have four moccasin soles, and the stranger said it was easy to make four moccasin soles from the two, for if the two soles were cut into halves, there would be four moccasins. The young man cut across his moccasin soles and made four pieces of them; but when he put his moccasins on, the soles would not spring, and he could travel no faster than he could before he had the magical moccasins. Then the stranger laughed loudly and long. When the young man asked him who he was, he said he was Iktomi, and that when the people told about the young man who went to get meat for the children they would laugh because he cut the soles of his moccasins.

Now the young man felt ashamed and he took his pouch of food into his hands, for that was all that was left of what the old woman had given him. When he took it in his hands it rattled like a rattle and he shook it toward Iktomi, causing Iktomi to flee in terror.

Then the young man laughed at Iktomi and went on his way toward the cave. When he came to the cave, he saw a new tipi beside it and stood looking at it. A beautiful young woman came out of it, took his hand, led him through the door and sat him on the man's seat in the tipi. She then sat at the woman's place finishing a pair of moccasins. The young man was so surprised that he only stared at her. When she had

finished the moccasins she said that now she had husbanded her tipi and had made moccasins for her man. So she gave them to the young man and bade him put them on. He did so and then he asked her who she was. She replied that she was his woman and would serve him as long as he would abide with her. He then told her that the children of his people cried for meat, that he was going to the west to learn how to get meat for them, and so could not stop and abide with her. She said that she had led him by the hand through the door of her tipi, seated him at the man's place in her tipi, and thus bound him to herself, and that by putting on the moccasins she had made for him he had consented to be her man, according to the customs of his people. The young man said that he could not let the little children of his people die of hunger, and that he must go and learn how to get meat for them. She replied that if he would abide with her in her tipi that night she would go with him and guide him to where he could learn how to get plenty of meat.

The young man stayed with her that night and in the morning they traveled together in the cave, she guiding. Thus, they came down to where the buffalo people live and found them dancing. The young woman gave her man a whistle and told him to dance with the buffalo people. He did so, learning how to dance as they did. Then his woman told him to sit with the musicians. He did so, learning the songs they sang.

When the dance was over the woman told the young man that the buffalo people had been dancing before the sun because they wished the sun to do something for them, and that when they please the sun in this manner, the sun would do that which they wished to be done. Then she took her man's hand and led

Sun Dance at the Rosebud Agency, from a photograph by Bert Bell taken in 1929. In the foreground (right) are dancers blowing on eagle bone whistlers, one carries a hoop, symbol of continuity (a recurrent theme in Lakota religion and mythology). The central figure is attached to the central dance pole by means of thongs that go to his chest. There is a concept of the transfer of power from the sacred pole to the dancer in spiritual dances of this type.

Piegan (a Blackfeet tribe) Medicine Men, Spotted Eagle, Chief Elk, and Bull Child, photographed prior to 1938 and showing part of the Sun Dance ceremony. The ethnologist J. C. Ewers identified them as 'Weather Dancers' who danced to ensure good weather during the ceremony. All three are inside the Sun Dance lodge, facing the central pole and blowing on their eagle wing bone whistles.

him to the tipi of the chief of the buffalo people and told her father that she had led this man though the door and seated him at the man's place in her tipi and that he had put on the moccasins she had made for him; that the little children of his people cried for meat, and he had come to learn how he could get meat for them. The chief told him that as he had accepted his daughter as his woman, he thus became the same as a buffalo man. Hence, the chief would tell how the buffalo people pleased the sun, so that the sun would give them what they wanted.

He said that when the people danced as they did when the young man came, it pleased the sun, and he would give what the people needed. He then told the young man to return to his people and tell them that if they would vow to dance before the sun when the snow was gone, and ask the sun for meat he would give

Two Lakota women: left, Rosie-Returns-from-Scout, right Nellie-No-Two-Horns, a relative of a famous Hunkpapa wood carver, who produced horse effigies replete with symbolism. The women wear magnificent dresses embellished with dentalium shells and carry shawls, so popular for this period.

them plenty of meat. The young man returned to his people and his woman went with him. He told his people all that he had seen and all that had been told him, and the people vowed to dance before the sun when the snow was gone. Then the shaman asked the sun to give them meat. Then the buffalo woman stood before the council and told them to have all the men prepare for killing game, and she would guide them to where they could kill enough to give plenty of meat.

When the women saw her stand before the council and heard her speak, they raised a great outcry, and said that she was the two-faced woman, and wanted to entice their men away from them, and called attention to her brown hair and blue eyes as proof that she was a wicked being. Then the men doubted her. The young man stood beside his woman and said he was wearing the moccasins she made for him, and he wrapped his robe about her and himself. He said there was meat for the little children, and if the men were afraid to go and bring it he would go with his woman to her people. Then the shaman stood before the people and they were silent. He filled and lighted a pipe and smoked it. Then he filled and lighted the pipe and passed it, and the council smoked in communion. While they smoked he made incense, first with sage, and then with sweetgrass.

Then he stood and the people were silent. He said that those who would not do as the young man had told them should suffer. Then the council ordered that all the men prepare as if for the chase and go, guided by the woman. She guided them to the other side of a hill and there they found a great herd of buffalo. The men killed until they were satisfied. The women had followed from the camp, wailing the songs that are sung for one who is departing on a perilous journey, but when they came to the top of the hill and saw the men killing, they hurried back to the camp, shouting and singing joyfully. They brought their implements and made meat of the dead buffalo.

Dakota woman preparing a large hide stretched on a wooden frame. Date not recorded, but probably circa 1900. This was a traditional method of softening large hides, another was to stake them on the ground. The hair and fatty tissue was carefully removed by the use of bone or horn tools. The softening process involved rubbing in the brains and liver of the animal and breaking the fibers by pulling the hide over a rawhide rope.

There was meat enough for many moons. The women prepared a great feast and when all were feasting the woman stood, and the women painted the parting of her hair red, and the shaman painted a red stripe across her forehead, thus making her the daughter of the people. The young man stood beside her, wrapping his robe about her and himself, and the young women sang songs in praise of them.

The raccoon moon came and the snow was gone and the people went their ways. Only the young man, his woman, and the shaman remained at the place of the winter camp. The young man sat with his robe over his head, for he had reminded the people of their vows to dance before the sun. They had replied that they had plenty of meat and soon they could hunt the buffalo and get more. Thus, the young man was ashamed for his people.

The people hunted, but found no game, and their meat was all gone. Then they remembered their vows, and came to ask the shaman what they should do. It was then the moon of ripe chokecherries. The shaman told the people that they had not been sincere when they vowed to the sun and that now they must manifest their sincerity by causing their blood to flow from wounds, and fulfill their vows by dancing before the sun; but, because the women had doubted that the sun would give meat they should not dance before the face of the sun. Then the buffalo woman showed the people how to make the camp circle and the dance lodge, and the young man taught the men the songs and the dance. The buffalo came and there was plenty of meat, and the woman showed the women how to prepare buffalo tongues for the feasts. The shaman told them how their blood must flow and how they must suffer because they had been insincere. When the moon was round all were ready, the women gave feasts and the men danced before the face of the sun and the sun was pleased. Since that time when a Lakota very much wishes for something he vows to dance the Sun Dance if the sun will give him what he wishes. If he does so he should dance the Sun Dance when the chokecherries are ripe.

THE SACRED BUNDLE
(*Pawnee*)

In the lodge or house of every Pawnee of influence, hanging on the west side, and so opposite the door, is the sacred bundle neatly wrapped in buckskin, and black with smoke and age. What these bundles contain we do not know. Sometimes, from the ends, protrude bits of scalps, and the tips of pipe stems and slender sticks, but the whole contents of the bundle are known only to the priests and to its owner, perhaps not always even to him. The sacred bundles are kept on the west side of the lodge, because, being thus furthest from the door, fewer people will pass by them than if they were hung in any other part of the lodge. Various superstitions attach to these bundles. In the lodges where certain of them are kept it is forbidden to put a knife in the fire, in others, a knife may not be thrown; in others, it is not permitted to enter the lodge with the face painted, or again, a man cannot go in if he has feathers tied in his head.

On certain sacred occasions the bundles are opened, and their contents form part of the ceremonial worship.

No one knows whence the bundles came. Many of them are very old; too old even to have a history. Their origin is lost in the haze of the long ago. The sacred bundles were given long ago. Noone knows when they came.

All the sacred bundles are from the far off country in the southwest, from which the Pawnees came long ago. They were handed down to the people before they started on their journey. Then they had never seen anything like iron, but they had discovered how to make the flint knives and arrow points. There was nothing that came to them through the whites. It all came through the power of Ti-ra'-wa. Through his power they were taught how to make bows and stone knives and arrow heads.

It was through the Ruler of the universe that the sacred bundles were given to them. They look to them, because through them and the buffalo and the corn, they worship Ti-ra'-wa. They all, even the chiefs,

A Pawnee man and woman who were keepers of the Skull Bundle associated with the southeast direction and the *Tcaihizparuxti* or 'Wonderful-Man' village of Pawnee mythology. The skull was said to be that of 'Closed-Man', a mythological leader who, before he died, directed that his skull be used in ceremonies so that he would be ever present with the Skidi Pawnee people.

LEFT *'Leader', a* Skidi *Pawnee priest, photographed probably by G. A. Dorsey, circa 1900. He was a prominent ritualist in the Morning Star ceremony and keeper of one of its important Bundles, the contents of which were believed to give communication between the Pawnee people and the supernatural powers. The ceremonies were to ensure ample food, long life, and prosperity for the tribe. Leader holds a large gourd rattle and an eagle feather fan.*

OPPOSITE *Ra tu tsa kntesa tu, or 'Sun Chief', a* Chaui *or Grand Pawnee, possibly photographed by W. H. Jackson, circa 1870. This man was a son of Petalesharro and was a chief and leader of the Pawnee councils. He wears a James Buchanan Peace medal dated 1857. Sun Chief's robe is embellished with star symbols; much of Pawnee ceremony centered around the heavenly bodies, particularly the Morning Star.*

respect the sacred bundles. When a man goes on the warpath, and has led many scouts and brought the scalps, he has done it through the sacred bundles. There were many different ceremonies that they used to go through. The high priest performs these ceremonies.

The high priestship was founded in this way: The black eagle spoke to a person, and said to him, "I am one of those nearest to Ti-ra'-wa, and you must look to me to be helped; to the birds and the animals – look to me, the black eagle, to the white headed eagle, to the otter and the buffalo."

The black eagle sent the buzzard as a messenger to this person, and he gave him the corn. The secrets of the high priestship and the other secrets were handed down at the same time. The buzzard, because he is bald, stands for the old men who have little hair. The white-headed eagle also represents the old men, those whose hair is white. These are the messengers through whom Ti-ra'-wa sends his words to the people. The Wichitas also had these secrets, and so have the Rees.

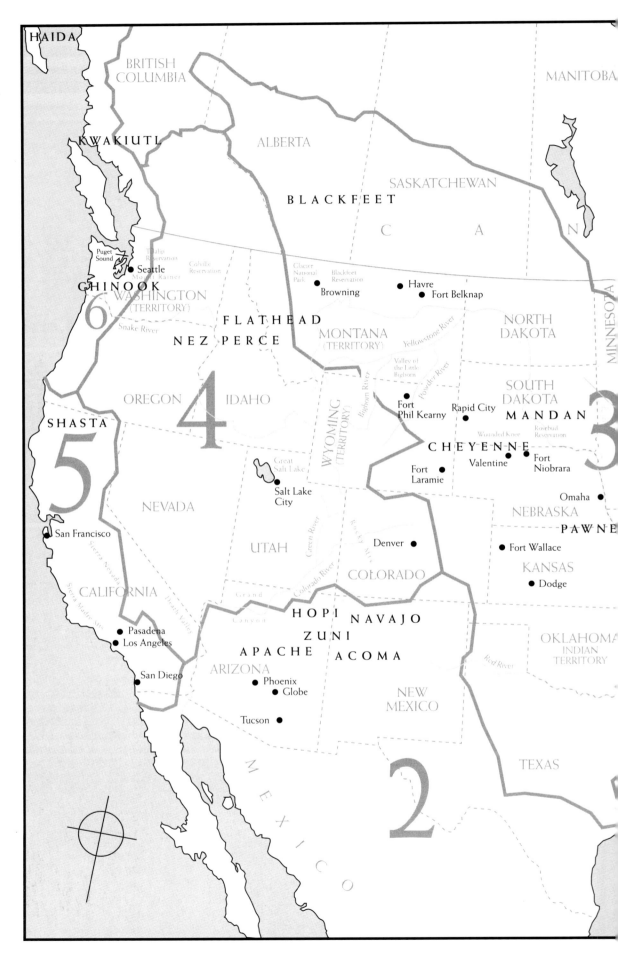

This map shows all the cultural areas and those tribes that have myths reproduced in the text. Modern boundaries have been included for ease of reference.

CHIPPEWA

ABENAKI
PASSAMAQUODDY

ONTARIO

QUEBEC

CANADA

HURON

SENECA
ONONDAGA
IROQUOIS

NEW YORK

New York

WISCONSIN

St Paul

Fort
Snelling

Red Lake

SIOUX

IOWA

Chicago

OHIO

INDIANA

PENNSYLVANIA

Philadelphia

Washington D C

WEST
VIRGINIA

VIRGINIA

Mississippi River

ILLINOIS

St Louis

8

MISSOURI

KENTUCKY

CHEROKEE

NORTH
CAROLINA

ARKANSAS

TENNESSEE

MUSKOGEE

SOUTH
CAROLINA

1

ALABAMA

GEORGIA

MISSISSIPPI

CHOCTAW

LOUISIANA

New Orleans

Fort Marion

FLORIDA

0   miles   300

1 The Southeast
2 The Southwest
3 The Plains
4 Plateau and Basin
5 California
6 The Northwest Coast
7 The Subarctic
8 The Northeast
9 The Arctic

ALASKA

9

AHTNA

KODIAK ISLAND

Glacier Bay

7

TLINGIT

6

0   miles   300

BIBLIOGRAPHY AND SUGGESTED FURTHER READING

BARBEAU, MARIUS, 'How The Raven Stole The Sun', *Transactions of the Royal Society of Canada*, third series, section II, vol. xxxvii, Ottawa, 1944

— 'Tsimsyan Myths', *National Museum of Canada, Bulletin*, no. 174, Ottawa, 1961

BARBEAU, M. and BENYON, W., *Tricksters, Shamans and Heroes: Tsimshian Narratives*, Ottawa, 1987

BARNETT, H.G., *The Coast Salish*, Eugene, Oregon, 1955

BOAS, F., 'Kwakiutl Culture as Reflected in Mythology', *Memoirs of the American Folk-Lore Society*, New York, 1935

BOWERS, A., *Mandan Social and Ceremonial Organization*, Chicago University Press, Chicago, 1950

BROTHERSTON, GORDON, *Image of the New World: The American Continent Portrayed in Native Texts*, Thames and Hudson, Ltd., London, 1979

BROWN, VINSON, *Voices of Earth and Sky*, Stackpole Books, Harrisburg, Pa., 1974

BRYANT, PAGE, *Native American Mythology*, Aquarian/Thorsons, London, 1991

BURLAND, COTTIE, *North American Indian Mythology*, Paul Hamlyn, London, 1965

CATLIN, GEORGE, *Letters and Notes on the Manners, Customs, and Condition of the North American Indians*, 2 vols, published by the author, at the Egyptian Hall, Piccadilly, London, 1841

— 'O-kee-pa': a Religious Ceremony and other Customs of the Mandans*, edited by John C. Ewers, Yale University Press, New Haven, 1967

CLARK, E. A., *Indian Legends of Canada*, Toronto, 1960

DENSMORE, FRANCES, 'Teton Sioux Music', *Bureau of American Ethnology, Bulletin*, no. 61, Smithsonian Institution, Washington, DC, 1918

DORSEY, GEORGE, *Pawnee Mythology*, Carnegie Institution of Washington, Washington, DC, 1977

DUTTON, B. and OLIN, C., *Myths and Legends of the Indians of the Southwest: Navajo, Pima, Apache: Book I*, Santa Barbara, California, 1991

— *Myths and Legends of the Indians of the Southwest: Hopi, Acoma, Tewa, Zuni: Book II*, Santa Barbara, California, 1991

EPPRIDGE, THERESA, 'The Star Image and Plains Indian Star Legends', *Plains Indian Design Symbology and Decoration*, edited by Gene Ball and George Horse Capture, Buffalo Bill Historical Center, Cody, Wyoming, 1980

ERDOES, R. and ORTIZ, A., *American Indian Myths and Legends*, New York, 1984

EWERS, J. C. (ed.), *Indian Art in Pipestone: George Catlin's Portfolio in the British Museum*, British Museum Press and Smithsonian Institution, London and Washington, DC, 1979.

GIFFORD, E. W., and BLOCK, G. H., *California Indian Nights Entertainment: Stories of the Creation of the World, of Man, of Fire, of the Sun, of Thunder*, Glendale, California, 1930

— *California Indian Nights Entertainment: Stories of Coyote, the Land of the Dead, the Sky Monsters, Animal People*, Glendale, California, 1930

HARDIN, TERRI (ed.), *Legends & Lore of the American Indians*, Barnes & Noble Books, New York, 1993

HELBIG, A. (ed.), *Nanabozho: Giver of Life*, Brighton, Michigan, 1987

HOWARD, JAMES H, 'The British Museum Winter Count'. *British Museum Occasional Paper No. 4*, Department of Ethnography, London, 1979

HULTKRANTZ, A., 'Mythology and Religious Concepts', *Handbook of North American Indians*, vol. ii, edited by W. L. D'Azevedo, Washington, D.C., 1986

IRVING, SUE AND HARPER, LYNETTE, 'Not Another Fur Trade Exhibit? An Inside Look at *Trapline Lifeline*', *Muse*, Autumn, 1988

LANKFORD, G. E. (ed.), *Southeastern Legends: Tales from the Natchez, Caddo, Biloxi, Chickasaw, and Other Nations*, Little Rock, Arkansas, 1987

LOWIE, ROBERT H., 'Myths and Traditions of the Crow Indians', *Anthropological Papers of the American Museum of Natural History*, vol. xxv, part I. New York, 1918 (Reprint: Bison Books, University of Nebraska Press, Lincoln and London. Introduction by Peter Nabokov, 1993)

McCLINTOCK, WALTER, *The Old North Trail* (Bison Book Reprint), University of Nebraska Press, Lincoln and London, 1968

MILLER, H, and HARRISON, E., *Coyote Tales of the Montana Salish*, Rapid City, South Dakota, 1974

MOONEY, JAMES, 'The Sacred Formulas of the Cherokees', *Annual Report of the Bureau of American Ethnology* (1885-86), Government Printing Office, Washington, DC, 1891, pp. 307-97

— 'The Ghost Dance Religion and Wounded Knee', *14th Annual Report (Part 2) of the Bureau of American Ethnology*, Smithsonian Institution, Washington, DC, 1896 (Reprint, Dover Publications Inc., New York, 1973)

MORRISEAU, N., *The Legends of my People, the Great Ojibway*, Toronto, 1965

NELSON, R. K., *Make Prayers to the Raven: A Koyukon View of the Northern Forest*, Chicago, 1983

PAPER, JORDAN, *Offering Smoke: The Sacred Pine and Native American Religion*, The University of Alberta Press, Edmonton, 1988

PARSONS, E. C., 'Micmac Folklore', *The Journal of American Folk-Lore*, no.38, Washinton, D.C., 1925

RASMUSSEN, K., 'The Netsilik Eskimos: Social Life and Spiritual Culture', *Report of the Fifth Thule Expedition, 1921-24*, vol. 8, parts 1-2, 1931

ROCKWELL, DAVID, *Giving Voice to Bear*, Roberts Rinehart Publishers, Colorado, 1991

SHEEHAN, CAROL, 'The Northwest Coast', *Native American Myths and Legends*, Salamander Books Ltd., London, 1994

SPECK, F. G., *The Celestial Bear Comes Down to Earth*, Reading, Pennsylvania, 1945

SPENCE, LEWIS, *The Myths of the North American Indians*, George G. Harrap & Company, London, 1916

— *The Illustrated Guide to North American Mythology*, introduction by Arthur Cotterell, Studio Editions, London, 1993

SWANTON, JOHN R., 'Indian Tribes of the Lower Mississippi Valley and Adjacent Coast of the Gulf of Mexico', *Bureau of American Ethnology, Bulletin*, no. 43, Smithsonian Institution, Washington, DC, 1911

— 'Source Material for the Social and Ceremonial Life of the Choctaw' Indians', *Bureau of American Ethnology, Bulletin*, no. 103, Smithsonian Institution, Washington, DC, 1931

TANNER, A., *Bringing Home Animals: Religious Ideology and Mode of Production of the Mistassini Cree Hunters*, New York, 1979

TAYLOR, COLIN F., 'Costume with Quill-wrapped Hair: Nez Perce or Crow?', *American Indian Art Magazine*, vol. vi, no. 3, Scottsdale, Arizona, 1981, pp. 42-53

— *The Plains Indians*, Salamander Books Ltd., London, 1994

— (ed.), *Native American Myths and Legends*, Salamander Books Limited, London, 1994

VOEGELIN, C. F. (trans.), *'Walam Olum' or 'Red Score': The Migration Legend of the Lenni Lenape or Delaware Indians*, Indiana Historical Society, Indianapolis, 1954

WALKER, J. R., 'The Sun Dance and other Ceremonies of the Oglala Division of the Teton Dakota', *Anthropological Papers of the American Museum of Natural History*, vol. xvi, part II, New York, 1917

— *Lakota Myth*, edited by Elaine A. Jahner, University of Nebraska Press, Lincoln and London, 1983

WEYER, E. M., *The Eskimos: Their Environment and Folkways*, New Haven, Connecticut, 1932

WISSLER, CLARK, 'Some Protective Designs of the Dakota', *American Museum of Natural History*, vol. i, part II, New York, 1907

WOOD, RAYMOND W. and LIBERTY, MARGOT (eds), *Anthropology on the Great Plains*, University of Nebraska Press, Lincoln and London, 1980

WOODHEAD, HENRY (ed.), *People of the Desert*, Time-Life Books, Alexandria, Virginia, 1993

FOOTNOTES TO CHAPTER INTRODUCTIONS

CHAPTER 2

1. While most pipes were of two pieces – the bowl and the stem – some ancient types, such as the War Pipe and that used in the Mandan O-kee-pa ceremony were of one piece and generally made of wood (see Paper).

2. Catlinite was a red stone quarried in Minnesota and first described by the artist and traveller, George Catlin (1796-1872), who visited the site in 1834. It is fairly soft when first dug out of the ground, hardens on exposure to air, and can be highly polished giving the appearance of red marble (see Catlin, 1841, vol. ii, pp. 201-6).

3. Spiders' webs were traditionally rubbed on the hands of young Navajoes to impart the same skillful qualities of the spider to the aspiring weavers.

CHAPTER 3

4. This is an interesting reference to feminism among the Pawnees: women of North American Indian societies actually held more power than is generally recognized (see, for example, K.M. Weist in Wood and Liberty (eds), pp. 255-71).

5. This the Pawnees continued to do until the custom was abandoned in about 1838. It was generally abhorred by most who were involved but carried out for fear of angering the gods.

CHAPTER 4

6. Picture-writing was widely practised and of ancient origin in North America, so-called 'Winter Counts' being used to record tribal events and history and documented among the eastern seaboard tribes as early as 1680 (Howard, p. 5).

7. In Sioux beadwork, the war-house was invariably worked in blue or green beads, obviously a reference to the sky from which the power of the lightning emanated.

CHAPTER 5

8. Wakan-Tanka, or the 'Great Spirit' in the language of the Lakota (Plains Sioux), probably comes closest to the Christian concept of God – a great power that pervaded the universe and was the creator of all things.

TEXT CREDITS

All efforts have been made to apply to copyright holders for permission to
reproduce text extracts and the publishers would like to thank the
following:

The Trustees of the British Museum, London, and the Smithsonian
Institution, Washington, DC (J. C. Ewers (ed.): *Indian Art in Pipestone:
George Catlin's Portfolio in the British Museum*, British Museum Press and
Smithsonian Institution, London and Washington, DC, 1979, caption
for plate 3)

The Trustees of the Smithsonian Institution, Washington, DC,
(J. R. Swanton: 'Source Material for the Social and Ceremonial Life of
the Choctaw Indians', *Bureau of American Ethnology, Bulletin*, no. 43,
Washington, DC, 1931, pp. 202-4),

University of Chicago (A. Bowers: *Mandan Social and Ceremonial Organization*,
Chicago, 1950, p. 365)

PICTURE CREDITS

All the black and white photographs in this book are published with the
premission of the National Anthropological Archive, Smithsonian
Institution, Washington, DC.

The artefacts reproduced in colour are all from the collection of Colin
Taylor in Hastings, England, and were photographed by Ian Fane.

INDEX

Numbers in italics refer to photographs